Society of Illustrators

ILLUSTRATORS 24

The 24th Annual of American Illustration

EXHIBITION HELD IN THE GALLERIES OF THE SOCIETY OF ILLUSTRATORS MUSEUM OF AMERICAN ILLUSTRATION,
128 EAST 63RD STREET, NEW YORK   FEBRUARY 3 - APRIL 14, 1982

1/24 PUBLISHED FOR THE SOCIETY OF ILLUSTRATORS BY MADISON SQUARE PRESS, INC., NEW YORK 10010
DISTRIBUTED BY ROBERT SILVER ASSOCIATES, NEW YORK 10016

SOCIETY OF ILLUSTRATORS, INC.
128 EAST 63RD STREET, NEW YORK, N.Y. 10021

ISBN-0-942604-00-8
Library of Congress Catalog Card Number 59-10849

Printed and bound in Tokyo, Japan by Dai Nippon Printing Co. Ltd. through DNP (America), Inc.

Distributors to the trade in the United States:
Robert Silver Associates, 95 Madison Avenue, New York, NY 10016

Distributors to the trade in Canada:
General Publishing Co. Ltd., 30 Lesmill Road, Don Mills, Ontario, Canada M3B 2T6

Distributed in Continental Europe, by:
Feffer and Simons, B.V., 170 Rijnkade, Weesp, Netherlands

Distributed throughout the rest of the world by:
Fleetbooks, S.A., c/o Feffer and Simons, Inc., 100 Park Avenue, New York, NY 10017

ROBERT HALLOCK, Designer   ART WEITHAS, Editor

ROBERT HALLOCK

1914-1982

This book is dedicated to the memory of Bob Hallock who designed the
first annual of American illustration, ILLUSTRATORS '59 and subsequent
annuals 18, 20, 21, 22, 23 and this one — 24.

His work over the years has included magazine, book, packaging, films,
murals, exhibits, advertising design and illustration. His ten years,
1965-1975, as founder, managing editor and art director of the quarterly
graphic arts and public affairs journal LITHOPINION won over 100 awards
for excellence, including the prestigious New York State Council on the
Arts Award, presented by Governor Rockefeller at the Metropolitan Museum
of Art. His short film LITHO U.S.A. is in the Museum of Modern Art's permanent
film collection. He has contributed to the Society of Illustrators
Air Force art program and designed seven commemorative issues for the
U.S. Postal Service.

The Society of Illustrators has lost a great contributing member and
a superb designer.

PRESIDENT'S MESSAGE

This book, the 24th Annual of American Illustration, is edited and published by the Society of Illustrators.

It is derived from a major exhibition of original art displayed in the Society of Illustrators Museum of American Illustration in New York. These 501 reproductions were judged the finest art of the previous year from over 6,000 entries in advertising, book, editorial, and institutional categories. A total of 36 distinguished artists and art directors comprised the four separate juries.

This volume features both published and unpublished works represented in their respective categories. Each category is introduced by the names and photographs of the jurors and the award winning illustrations.

The Society of Illustrators, as a public service, educational organization, thus continues its annual tradition of presenting the best contemporary illustration to an increasingly aware public, to artists, art buyers, art directors, and educators and art students.

John Witt
President

Arthur Weithas
Editor

JURYING THE ANNUAL EXHIBITION: HOW IT WORKS

The most important function of the Annual Exhibition Past Chairmen's Committee is the selection of jurors which takes place approximately seven months prior to the actual jurying.

A large blackboard is set up with five vertical columns — four for the categories (Advertising, Editorial, Book & Institutional) and one in which to list diverse types of jurors. Every effort is made to create a good mix of illustrators and art directors with a wide range of tastes.

The first jurors selected are four Society of Illustrators members, each of whom acts as chairman of one of the categories. Eight additional jurors, including non-Society members, are then selected for each category. In order to avoid bias, jurors are placed in categories other than those from which their primary income is derived professionally. A period of three years must elapse before a juror may

serve again. Jurors may not win awards in the category they are judging.

Jurying takes place during four evenings in October — one category a night. All published entries are set out in piles of black and white, 2-color, full color, and are also broken down according to size within that framework. After the jurors have completed viewing all the entries and have marked those which they feel qualify for the show, the staff sorts them into groups of "like" votes and those with the highest are brought back to be considered for awards.

During the initial voting, jurors are asked to vote silently, without discussion, but when the selection of awards gets underway, jurors are invited to express their views on why they think a certain piece merits an award.

The unpublished entries, submitted in slide form, are projected on a screen and

voted on by means of a unique voting machine which enables each juror to cast his vote privately. Awards for unpublished pieces are selected the following week by the Balancing Jury.

The Balancing Jury is composed of the four Category Chairmen and two Past Chairmen. Since each artist accepted in the show is allowed no more than three pieces in a category and no more than five in the entire show (not counting award-winning pieces), it is the Balancing Jury's responsibility to whittle down those exceeding this number.

The Society of Illustrators takes great pride in the integrity with which this show has been run over the years and intends to maintain this high standard.

Arpi Ermoyan
Executive Director

HALL OF FAME AWARD

As the name implies, the Hall of Fame Awards are presented by the Society of Illustrators each year to those artists who have made an outstanding contribution to the art of illustration.

The list is long and impressive and the recipients are the greatest illustrators of the past and present. The first award was made in 1958 to Norman Rockwell.

This year's award winners are Eric (Carl Erickson), the internationally famous Vogue artist; Henry Raleigh, the great and prolific contributor to the Saturday Evening Post (both awarded posthumously) and John Clymer, the superb painter-recorder of the western scene.

Hall of Fame Chairman: Willis Pyle
Hall of Fame Committee:
Past Presidents of the Society
Walter Brooks
Henry Carter
Stevan Dohanos
Tran Mawicke
Charles McVicker
John A. Moodie
Howard Munce
Alvin J. Pimsler
Warren Rogers
William Schneider
Shannon Stirnweis
David K. Stone
Harold von Schmidt

**HALL OF FAME, 1982
ERIC (Carl Erickson)
(1891-1958)**

Photograph by Irving Penn. Vogue December 1949.
Copyright ©1949 (renewed 1977) by The Condé Nast Publications Inc.

It is an interesting fact that the two artists honored posthumously by induction into The Society of Illustrators Hall of Fame were both superb draftsmen in the classic tradition of observation and delineation.

They were friends and each admired the ability of the other.

In point of difference, Eric's drawings expressed his belief that "more is less" while Raleigh believed the opposite, "more is better". Their work is testimony to their credo.

In the twenties, fashion and society were wrapped up in one beautiful package and presented in Vogue Magazine in the New York, Paris and London editions. What Vogue reported, Eric depicted with sophis-

tication, style and honesty.

His association with Vogue continued for over three decades as fashion artist, portraitist and reporter.

A word from Vogue could make or break a collection and the famous designers, Mainbocher, Chanel, Schiaparelli, Dior and Yves St. Laurent vied to have Eric draw their fashions. He recorded them with keen observation of essential detail and with distinction, style and grace.

He portrayed the great and the near great of the period — Gertrude Stein, Collette, Edith Piaf, Toscanini and Franklin Roosevelt. He drew them all with a discerning eye, recognizing the revealing features that denoted their character.

In reportage, whether it was a speak-

easy in New York, a day at the races at Longchamps, the bombshelters of London or G.I.'s asleep in wartime Grand Central Station, he caught the importance of gestures in compositions that told the complete story simply and succinctly.

He *suggested* completion. He allowed *you* into his drawing.

While his drawings appeared deceptively artless they were painstakingly arrived at. He drew with the music of Chopin or Debussy as background while the model gradually wilted under the sustained pressure of holding a long pose. He drew only what he saw.

Through his long association with Vogue (1925 until his death in 1958), he gained an international reputation as an artist, as well known in Paris as here. He was referred to as "the Toulouse-Lautrec of America". He maintained studios both in New York and in Paris.

Diana Vreeland recalls that Eric was a boulevardier in the true sense of the word. He was a keen observer of life and fortunately for us he was able to record his observations with honesty and sophistication.

Felix Topolski said "Eric's draftsmanship impressed me: its unerring simplicity, unostentatious color, its seriousness. I never saw a single drawing of his which did not carry his sense of responsibility, as it were, toward his duty as a recorder of a scene or the shape of a dress."

Jean Cocteau said: "Carl Erickson reigned in an antic world where the droll sometimes takes on the strength of trag-edy. I testify to my admiration of his work."

Carl Oscar August Erickson was born in Joliet, Illinois (1891) of Swedish parents. He was a disinterested student. His early interests as a boy were drawing and boxing. He made endless sketches in the gym. He was called "Eric" in art school in Chicago and the name stuck. He adopted it as his signature.

Physically, he bore a striking resemblance to Robert Benchley, the humorist ... small in stature, he jauntily sported a bowler, a cane and a cornflower boutonniere. He was always impeccably groomed. His brown eyes were set in slightly puffy sockets. Laugh lines creased a round face and a closely cropped mustache partly hid a wry smile. At his favorite restaurants he was referred to as "Monsieur Le Baron".

Eric had the unusual honor of having a major exhibition at the Brooklyn Museum of Art in 1959 posthumously. He is represented in the New Britain Museum of American Illustration, The Society of Illustrators Museum of American Illustration and numerous private collections.

He lived in the Grand Manner and drew the life he lived with elegant sophistication and taste.

It is no wonder that the appeal of Eric's drawing has engendered a growing cult of illustrators and students who appreciate the talent of "Eric", the boulevardier from Joliet, Illinois.

Art Weithas

HENRY PATRICK RALEIGH

The craft he learned as a newspaper reporter required a keen eye, a remarkable memory and a sense of "something about to happen". Raleigh realized the importance of this experience when he said, "Contemporary illustrators might consider with some envy the perspective genius of their predecessors whose contact with life was intimate before the camera and its second hand authority." A natural draftsman, he disdained the camera.

His exposure through the vast combined circulation of the Post, Harper's Bazaar and Hearst's International made him famous and his prolific production made him wealthy. He was able to indulge his fondness for yachts and travel. To Raleigh, "travel restored the fresh childlike enthusiasm, naivete and spontaneity which is absolutely necessary if art is going to mean anything." His sketches of these journeys and his rare etchings were not executed

HALL OF FAME, 1982
HENRY PATRICK RALEIGH
(1880-1944)

Henry Patrick Raleigh was a superb natural draftsman in the classic tradition of F.R. Gruger and Wallace Morgan. He was a "star" during the Golden Age of American Illustration (1900-1930).

His graceful, fluid drawings, usually of crowded social scenes, were done in line, wash or colored inks and seemed to flow from his fingertips.

Born of Irish parents in Portland, Oregon, he moved to San Francisco at the age of twelve and got a job as a shipping clerk in a coffee concern in order to help support his mother and sister. The head of the firm became impressed by his drawing ability and sent him to Hopkins Academy in San Francisco to study art.

At seventeen, he was hired by the San Francisco Chronicle as a cub reporter-artist covering such assignments as fires, floods and "promising young corpses" at the morgue to illustrate the latest murder or suicide. He later did graphic reporting on the Spanish-American War and the Klondike Gold Rush.

By nineteen, he was working for the San Francisco Examiner, William Randolph Hearst's favorite newspaper, as one of their highest paid artists. From there, it was just a short step to New York and work on Hearst's Journal and assignment on other magazines.

until his return home — a tribute to his powers of observation and memory.

A serious etcher, he produced many fine plates. He was awarded the Shaw Prize for illustration from the Salmagundi Club in 1916 and the Gold Medal for Advertising Art in America in 1926.

Home to Raleigh was what is now the famous artists' colony of Westport, Conn. He, George Wright, Frederick Dorr Steele and Rose O'Neill helped pioneer that area's popularity. However, Raleigh spent a large part of his life in seclusion in his Gramercy Park studio.

It was in this "illustration a day" studio that he distinguished himself "by his ability to depict a large group of people in an interior with refinement and grace". His classic campaign for Maxwell House Coffee, commissioned by the J. Walter Thompson Advertising Agency, depicted dramatic scenes of Southern Ante-Bellum society, set in elaborate homes.

Raleigh believed, and his drawings proved, that illustrators are artists in the broadest sense of the word. His newspaper experience and its discipline, his appreciation for Forain and Daumier's incisive interpretation of character all helped to develop his individual style.

His fame brought sadness to the story of this outstanding artist. He lived a life style he thought would never end. While he delineated a social scene of gaiety and elegance, he himself grew morose and introverted. Unable to adapt to illustration's new market and not willing to accept the social mores of the late 30's and 40's, his spirit cracked and, in 1944, Raleigh took his own life.

His art, however, has never paled and he remains a giant from the era of the Golden Age of American Illustration.

Terrence Brown

Illustration for Maxwell House Coffee, Collection of the Society of Illustrators Museum of American Illustration

HALL OF FAME, 1982
JOHN CLYMER

Photo Courtesy of Artist

The big turning point in John Clymer's life came when he first saw a reproduction of a painting by Frank Schoonover done for a Brown & Bigelow calendar. On the back was a biographical sketch of the artist which included the artist's address. Not only did he carefully fold and save the reproduction for future reference, but it gave focus to a lifelong goal. As a youngster growing up in the small mountain town of Ellenville, Washington, John was inspired by the wilderness and wanted to make pictures of the wildlife around him, but he had no idea how to go about it. Now he knew he wanted to be an illustrator.

Enrolling in a correspondence course, Clymer learned the rudiments of working for reproduction, and by the time he finished he had made his first sale to the pulp magazines. However, he realized he did not know enough and began an impossible 18-hour day study program. He had a daytime job in a studio making clothing catalog drawings, went to art school at night, and studied privately with Vancouver artist, George Southwell, until 2 a.m. After two years of this, John's health broke down. At the age of twenty, he was a physical wreck. His doctor advised a complete change of scene, normal hours, and some hard physical labor. John took a job offer as a deck hand on a paddle wheeler making a trip up to the Yukon. It was rugged work but also an opportunity to know the life of the Indians and trappers along the way. This became a rich mine of information for his later career. As John says, "I never planned it that way, but that chance summer's trip has guided and shaped my life since."

Back in Vancouver, John wondered what he should do next. On impulse, he took out Frank Schoonover's address and without prior announcement made the long trip to Wilmington, Delaware, to seek advice. Schoonover sent him back for fur-

John Clymer "Grand Parade — Green River Rendezvous 1836" Private Collection

ther study in Vancouver where he was already illustrating for Canadian publications.

It took a longer time to break into the American magazines. Subsequent study with Harvey Dunn played a big part in preparing him for the intensively competitive New York market.

However, the emphasis in the magazines was on boy-girl romances which was not Clymer's forte. Doing them was a painful struggle. The direction of his career was changed by a stint as a Marine Corps artist during World War II.

After the war, he began to do covers for THE SATURDAY EVENING POST with requirements much more suited to his own outlook and for several years Clymer's cover paintings of regional Americana were extremely popular subjects with the public.

Simultaneously, the artist was painting and exhibiting historical illustrations, par-

ticularly of situations relating to the Oregon Trail and settlement of the West. Based on family diaries, visits to the actual sites of events and with thorough research in area museums, his paintings became authentic recreations of history never previously depicted. As John says, "Being on the spot where an event has occurred is much different than just reading about it. Going and seeing the places makes history come alive for me."

His gallery sold his historical pictures as soon as he painted them. Finding this new market meant that Clymer could drop his commercial work and paint pictures of his own choice. He then decided to move to Wyoming to be closer to his subject matter, with a studio located in the Tetons. There he can see deer and elk from his window, and many of his finest pictures have been painted in this studio.

Today John Clymer is one of the most esteemed painters of the historic West. He

had done an important mural for the Whitney Gallery of Western Art in Cody, Wyoming, and his paintings hang in important public and private collections across the country.

With the organization of the Cowboy Artists of America and the National Academy of Western Art, Clymer was embraced by both groups and his pictures have won top honors from each in their annual exhibitions. Despite his own modestly stated objectives, "All I wanted to do was live in the mountains and paint," John Clymer has created an important and authentic documentation of forgotten places and historical events that will now be remembered because he painted them.

Walt Reed

HAMILTON KING AWARD

The Hamilton King Award is given each year for the finest illustration by a member of the Society of Illustrators.
The 1982 award winner is Robert Heindel for one of a series of ballet paintings.

Hamilton King Award Jurors:

Ray Ameijide	Leo & Diane Dillon
Dave Blossom	Gerald McConnell
Paul Calle	Wilson McLean
Alan E. Cober	William Teason

HAMILTON KING AWARD WINNERS

1965	PAUL CALLE	1974	FRED OTNES
1966	BERNIE FUCHS	1975	CAROL ANTHONY
1967	MARK ENGLISH	1976	JUDITH JAMPEL
1968	ROBERT PEAK	1977	LEO & DIANE DILLON
1969	ALAN COBER	1978	DANIEL SCHWARTZ
1970	RAY AMEIJIDE	1979	WILLIAM TEASON
1971	MIRIAM SCHOTTLAND	1980	WILSON McLEAN
1972	CHARLES SANTORE	1981	GERALD McCONNELL
1973	DAVE BLOSSOM	1982	ROBERT HEINDEL

Rose and Robert Heindel

Photo By J. Berry O'Rourke

HAMILTON KING AWARD 1982
ROBERT HEINDEL

Evidently, Bob Heindel likes women. To be precise, there is one woman, a dark beauty, whose image is indelibly connected to his work — his wife of 24 years. He says of her, "Rose has had a profound effect on my work." In discussing his series of paintings entitled, "Notes to a Flower," he expands the thought, "I paint erotic images which depend on how I view her." In addition to this group of pictures and poetry, Rose's posing for Bob helps to solve problems for clients of every description. We see her suspended, dreaming over Wamsutta sheets, under elegant coverlets in annual reports, in naked tension for pharmaceutical ads. Her limbs are scattered on a table, a symbolic feast, in a piece for *Viva Magazine,* and, on the darker side, as a lyrically twisted corpse to illustrate a Playboy Book Club mystery.

It is not surprising that his lovely wife has effected his growth as an artist and a man. He and Rose knew each other as children in Toledo, Ohio where he was born in 1938. By 16 Bob knew what he wanted, so he enrolled in the Famous Artists School. The following year he felt confident enough to come to New York where he stayed at the 42nd Street "Y" when he wasn't showing his neophyte portfolio. The art directors sent him home. He continued his studies with some major interruptions. He married Rose and had two sons, Toby and Troy. They moved to Akron where Bob drew tires — another inducement to improve his skills, then to Denver to start an art studio. The next stop was Detroit where Bob did car ad backgrounds at Newcenter Studio and added Todd to the family. He finally completed the FAS course and risked New York again. This time they weren't smirking·at a raw kid. They were giving him jobs: Saturday Evening Post, Redbook, Ladies' Home Journal and Sports Illustrated. The Heindels finally settled into a beautiful, old farmhouse in Connecticut.

Bob considers his progression to becoming one of the most highly respected and rewarded illustrators as "normal," as if his abilities and continued artistic growth did not remove him from the crowd. "The business has been very good to me. I like the idea of communicating to 10 million people in *Time Magazine*, it's an ego trip." And he likes working for most of his many clients. Of them he says, "People generally know they have to let me do what I do, otherwise, they wouldn't call." But they've called and keep calling. Influenced by artists as diverse as Austin Briggs and Francis Bacon, his elegant lines and unusual compositions have rendered Steinbeck Oakies, Psychos and Sybils, Fonda, "Tommy" and Tatem, basketball players and ballet dancers.

Especially ballet dancers. This year's Hamilton King Award is for the exquisite painting for the Dallas Ballet Company. This deceptively simple image describes the extraordinary grace of two dancer's backs. It is a clear idea that comes from total immersion by the artist into the form. Three years ago the Atlanta Ballet asked Bob to do a poster which began an odyssey that continues. "Dance suits my style; it's sexy and beautiful. Dancers are a race unto themselves, they work a lot harder than I do." His appreciation of them has led to over 80 paintings and to shows in Atlanta, Kansas City, Houston and Dallas, timed to coincide with the opening of each company's season.

In addition to the ballet series, illustration jobs — many of which were SI annual show award winners, involvement with the prestigious Illustrators Workshop and the Famous Artists School — as their star graduate, he still has time to fly to the islands with Rose to play with the same intensity with which he works. As he says, "I still do exactly what I want to do."

Jill Bossert

"Two Ballet Dancers" Illustration for The Dallas Ballet Company

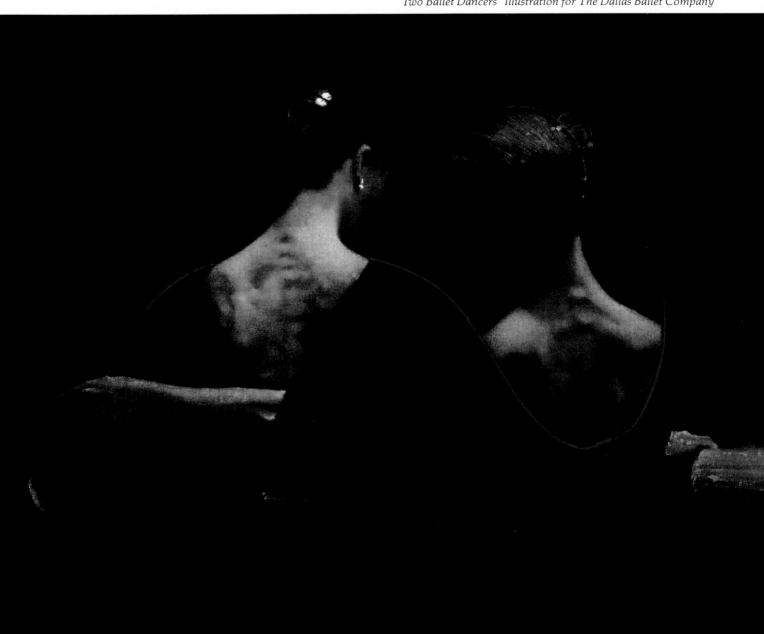

EDITORIAL

Local Programs May 30-June 5, 1981

TV GUIDE

40¢

How the
Gay Lobby Has
Changed TV
Page 2

Dan Rather

1
Artist: **BERNIE FUCHS**
Art Director: Jerry Alten
Client: TV Guide
GOLD MEDAL

2
Artist: **CHARLES A. BOIE**
Client: National Bus Trader, Inc.
GOLD MEDAL

3
Artist: **DANIEL SCHWARTZ**
Art Director: Rudolph Hoglund
Magazine:Time

4
Artist: **AARON SHIKLER**
Art Director: Rudolph Hoglund
Magazine:Time

5
Artist: **DANIEL MAFFIA**
Art Director: Nigel Holmes
Magazine:Time

6
Artist: **DANIEL MAFFIA**
Art Directors: Robert Best/Roger Black
Magazine: New York

7 Artist: **ROBERT A. OLSON**   Art Director: Barb Koster   Magazine:Passages

8 Artist: **LINDA CROCKETT-HANZEL**   Art Director: Greg Paul   Magazine:Cleveland Plain Dealer Magazine   **GOLD MEDAL**

9
Artist: **BRAD HOLLAND**
Art Directors: Tom Staebler/Kerig Pope
Magazine: Playboy

10   Artist: **STANLEY ROBERTS**

Landru case
1921

11 Artist: **MARTIN PATE**

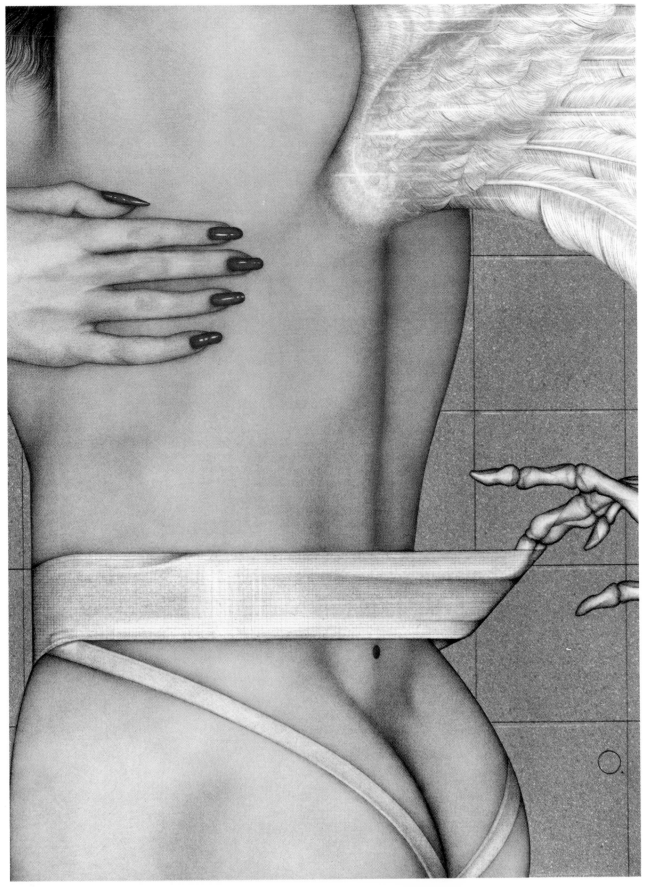

13 Artist: **MEL ODOM**   Art Directors: Tom Staebler/Kerig Pope   Magazine: Playboy   **GOLD MEDAL**

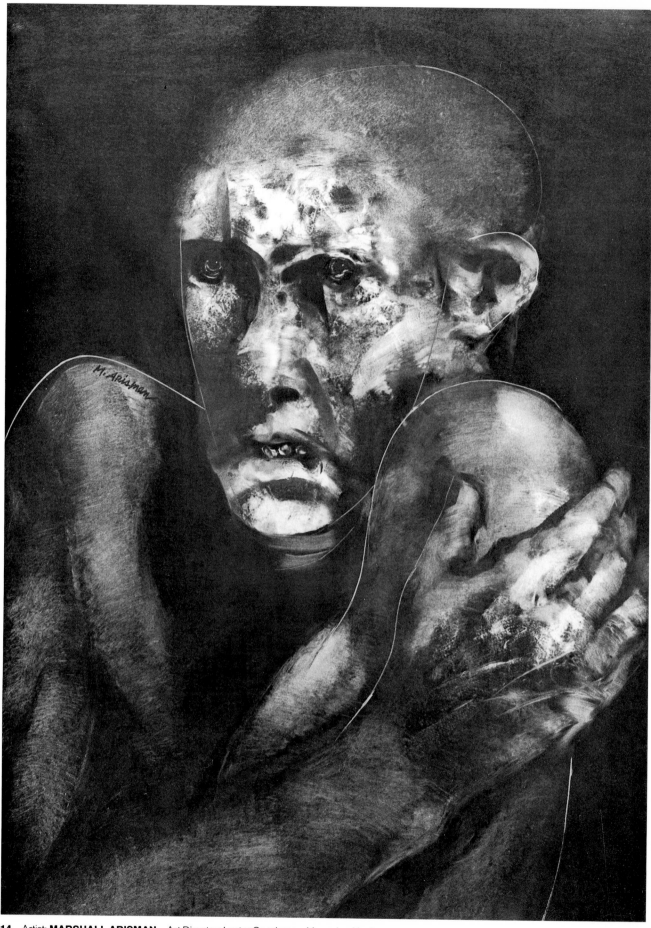

14 Artist: **MARSHALL ARISMAN** Art Director: Lester Goodman Magazine:Next

15 Artist: **MARSHALL ARISMAN** Art Director: Rudolph Hoglund Magazine:Time

16 Artist: **JOHN BERKEY**
SILVER MEDAL

17 Artist: **BERNIE FUCHS** Art Director: Richard Gangel Magazine:Sports Illustrated

18
Artist: **BRAD HOLLAND**
Art Directors: Tom Staebler/Bob Post   Magazine: Playboy

19
Artist: **MEL ODOM**
Art Directors: Tom Staebler/Kerig Pope
Magazine: Playboy

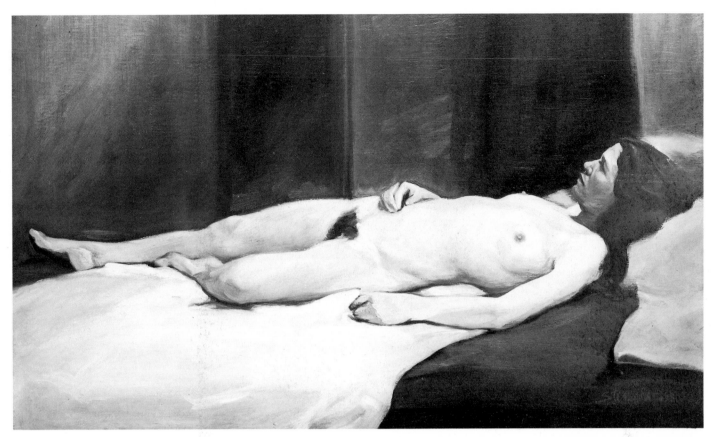

20 Artist: **KATHLEEN STEMELO**

21 Artist: **MARA McAFEE**

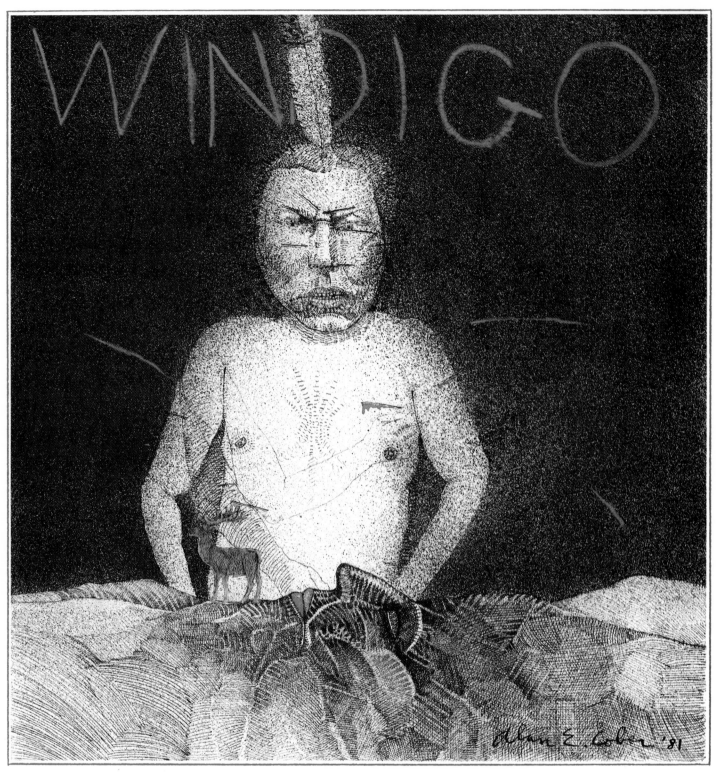

22 Artist: **ALAN E. COBER** Art Director: Mary Zisk Magazine:Science Digest

23
Artist: **MARSHALL ARISMAN**
Art Director: Joe Brooks
Magazine:Penthouse

24   Artist: **GREG MORAES**

25   Artist: **JIM SHARPE**   Art Director: Charlie Thompson   Client: ABC (20/20)

26
Artist: **DAVID NOYES**
Art Director: Joseph Kozlakowski
Client: across the board

27 Artist: **SKIP LIEPKE**   **PAST CHAIRMEN'S SPECIAL AWARD**

28 Artist: **ROBERT HEINDEL** Art Director: Tina Adamek Magazine: Postgraduate Medicine

29
Artist: **DENNIS MUKAI**
Art Directors: Tom Staebler/Len Willis
Magazine: Playboy

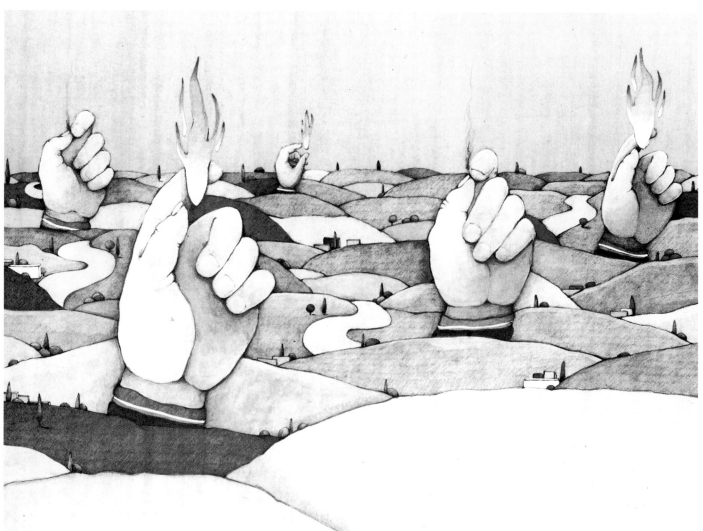

30 Artist: **DAGMAR FRINTA**   Art Director: Tom Lennon   Magazine: Emergency Medicine

31 Artist: **DEBBI CHABRIAN**   Art Director: Jean Karl   Client: Atheneum Publishers

32 Artist: **PETER FIORE** Art Director: Nina Scerbo Magazine: McCall's Working Mother

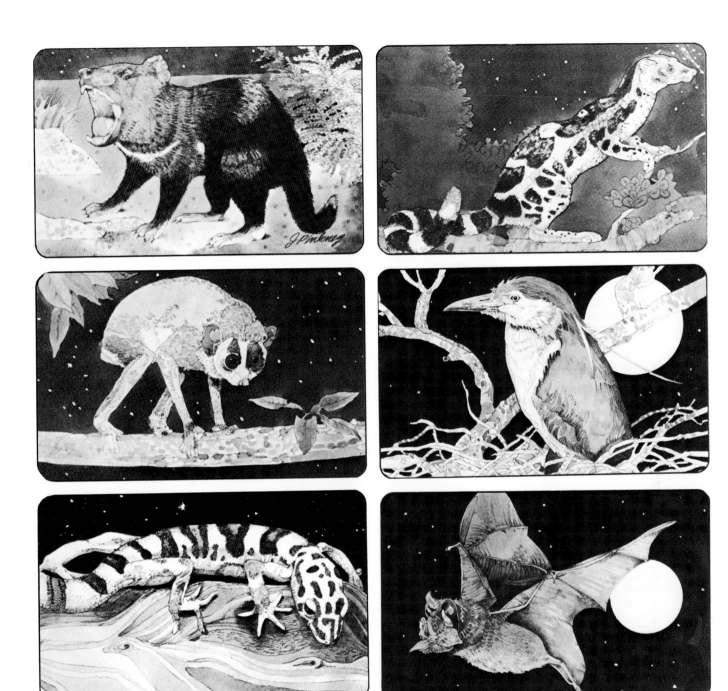

33
Artist: **JERRY PINKNEY**
Art Director: Al Nagy
Magazine: Contact

34 Artist: **BOB DACEY**   Art Director: Sal Barracca   Magazine: Ladies' Home Journal

35 Artist: **RONALD De FELICE**

36 Artist: **DENNIS LUZAK**   Art Director: Modesto Torre   Magazine: McCall's

37
Artist: **ROBERT McGINNIS**
Art Director: Sal Barracca
Magazine: Ladies' Home Journal

38 Artist: **ROBERT A. OLSON** Art Director: Tina Adamek Magazine: Postgraduate Medicine

39
Artist: **ROBERT ANDREW PARKER**
Art Director: Alfred Zelcer
Client: Trans World Airlines

40   Artist: **R. MICHAEL PALAN**

41
Artist: **PAUL MELIA**
Art Director: Kathy Turner
Client: Victory Theatre

42 Artist: **MICHAEL DUDASH** Art Director: Modesto Torre Magazine: McCall's

43 Artist: **FRANK MORRIS**   Art Director: Murry Keith   Magazine: Memphis

44
Artist: **ROBERT HEINDEL**
Art Director: Joe Connolly
Magazine: Scouting

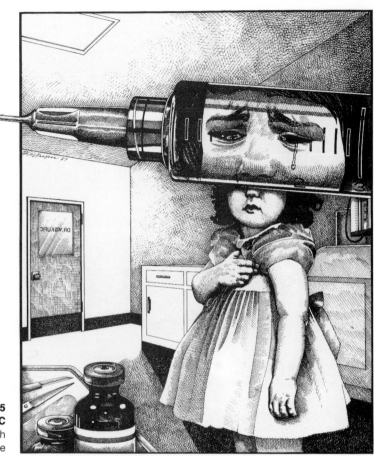

45
Artist: **GARY VISKUPIC**
Art Director: Miriam Smith
Publication: The Newsday Magazine

46 Artist: **CONNIE CONNALLY**

47 Artist: **JIM SPANFELLER** Art Director: Herb Lubalin Client: ITC

48 Artist: **DAGMAR FRINTA** Art Director: Nina Scerbo Magazine: McCall's Working Mother

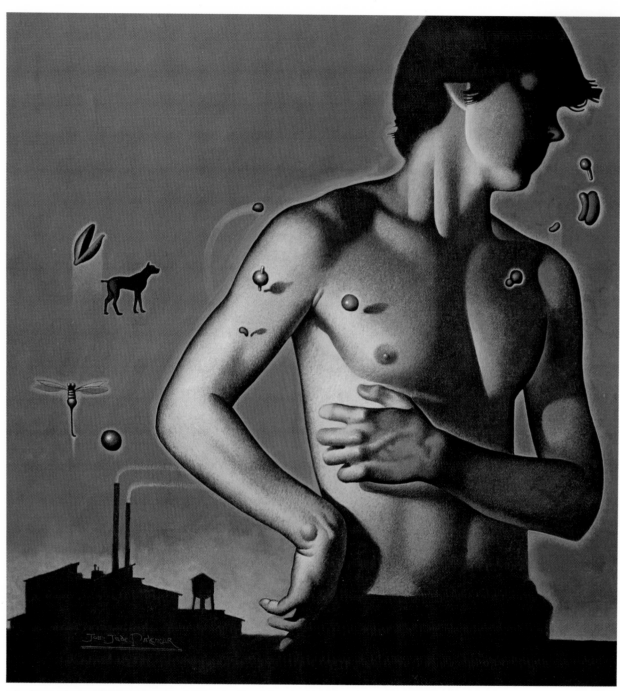

49 Artist: **JOHN JUDE PALENCAR**   Art Director: Tina Adamek   Magazine: Postgraduate Medicine

50 Artist: **DAVID GAMBALE** Art Director: Tina Adamek Magazine: Postgraduate Medicine

51
Artist: **CHRIS SPOLLEN**
Art Director: Alice Deganhardt
Magazine: Creative Living

52
Artist: **BRAD HOLLAND**
Art Directors: Tom Staebler/Bruce Hansen
Magazine: Playboy

53 Artist: **MARCIA MARX**   Art Director: Kerig Pope   Magazine: Playboy

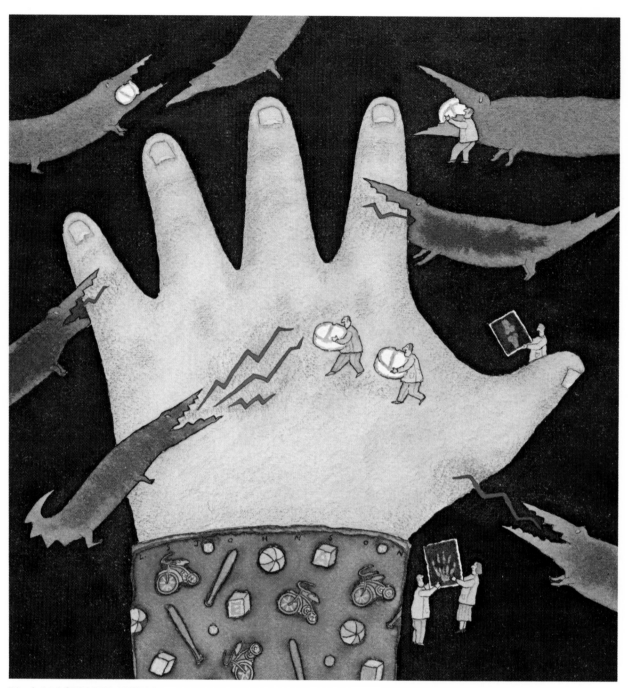

54 Artist: **LONNI SUE JOHNSON** Art Director: Tina Adamek Magazine: Postgraduate Medicine

55 Artist: **TOM EVANS** Art Director: Fred Woodward Magazine: D

56
Artist: **HARVEY DINNERSTEIN**
Art Director: Judy Garlan
Magazine: The Atlantic Monthly

57
Artist: **MARVIN MATTELSON**
Art Director: Rudolph Hoglund
Magazine: Time

58
Artist: **LINDA CROCKETT-HANZEL**
Art Director: Margot Letourneau
Magazine: Yankee

59 Artist: **JOHN COLLIER** Art Director: Alfred Zelcer Client: Trans World Airlines

60 Artist: **JOHN RUSH** Art Director: Carveth Kramer Magazine: Psychology Today

61 Artist: **NORMAN WALKER**   Art Director: Paula Jo Smith   Client: Literary Guild

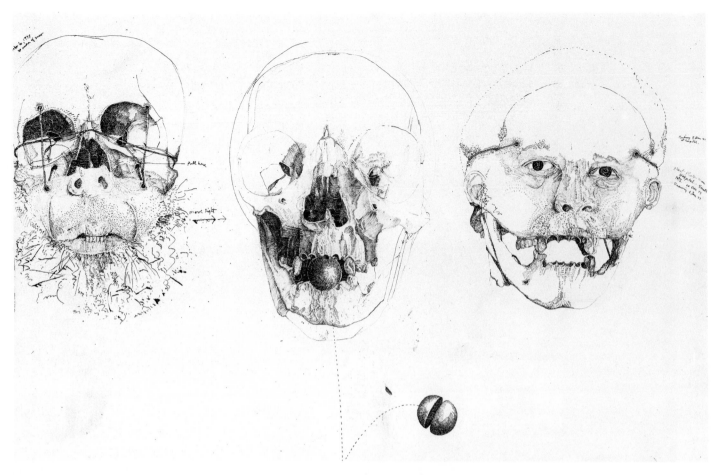

62
Artist: **ALAN E. COBER**
Art Director: Herb Lubalin
Magazine: U&lc

63
Artist: **ALAN E. COBER**
Art Director: Herb Lubalin
Magazine: U&lc

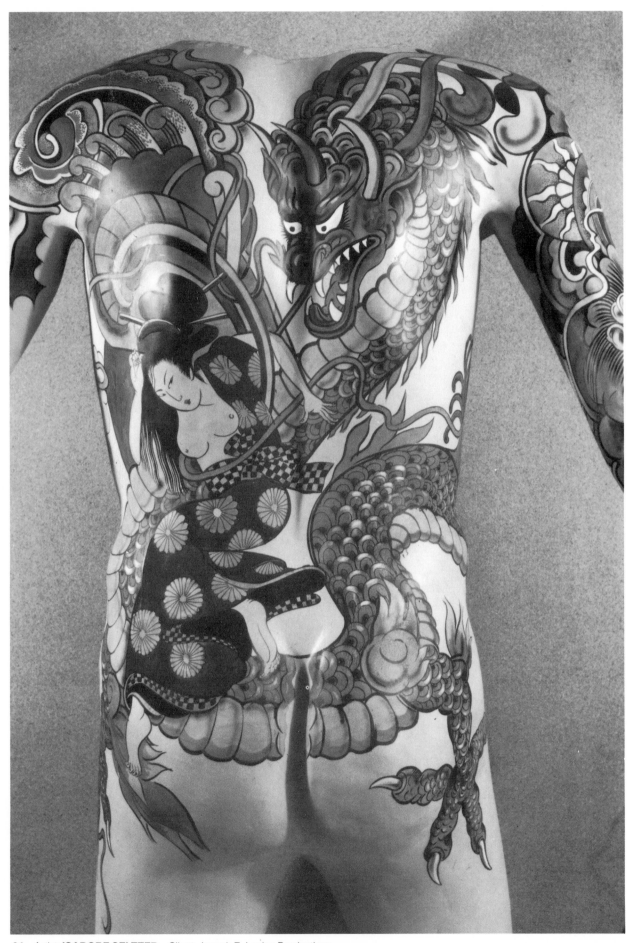

64 Artist: **ISADORE SELTZER** Client: Joseph E. Levine Productions

65
Artist: **FRED OTNES**
Art Director: Joe Connolly
Magazine: Boys' Life

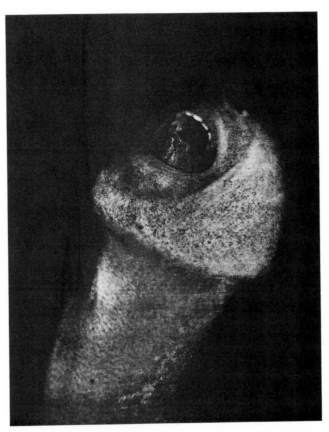

66   Artist: **ARTURO HERRERA**

67 Artist: **MARVIN MATTELSON**   Art Director: Rudolph Hoglund   Magazine: Time

68
Artist: **GERRY GERSTEN**
Art Director: Thomas R. Lunde
Magazine: Newsweek

69
Artist: **RICHARD SPARKS**
Art Director: Rudolph Hoglund
Magazine: Time

70

Artist: **ROBERT GOLDSTROM**

Art Director: Tom Lennon

Magazine: Emergency Medicine

71 Artist: **BRALDT BRALDS**   Art Directors: Maxine Davidowitz/Joy Toltzis Makon   Magazine: Redbook

72 Artist: **DAVID LEVINE** Art Director: Alfred Zelcer Client: Trans World Airlines

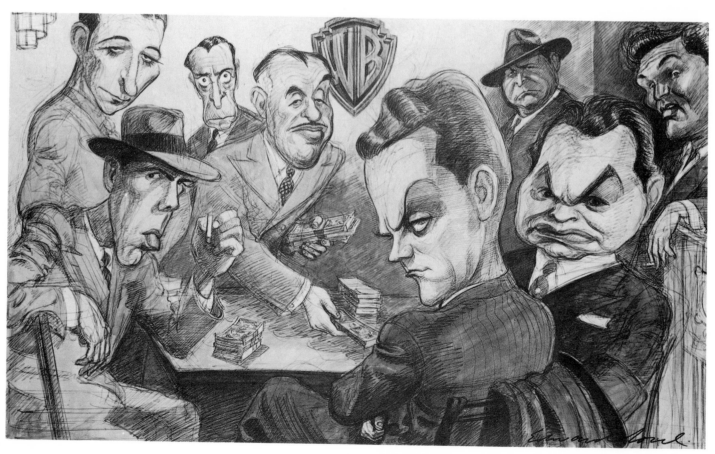

73 Artist: **EDWARD SOREL** Art Director: Walter Bernard Client: N.Y. Film Review

74 Artist: **WILLIAM A. MOTTA**

75 Artist: **BRALDT BRALDS** Art Director: Michael Brock Magazine: Oui

76 Artist: **GARY KELLEY**   Art Director: Fred Woodward   Magazine: D   **SILVER MEDAL**

77 Artist: **KATHLEEN STEMELO**

78 Artist: **BOB DAVIS**

79
Artist: **R. J. SHAY**
Art Director: Steve McKinstry
Client: Seattle Times

80 Artist: **BURT SILVERMAN**   Art Director: Carveth Kramer   Magazine: Psychology Today

81 Artist: **JACK PARDUE** Art Director: Howard Larkin Magazine: Listen

82   Artist: **ROBERT M. CUNNINGHAM**

83 Artist: **WILSON McLEAN**   Art Director: Joe Brooks   Magazine: Penthouse

84 Artist: **BART FORBES**   Art Director: Anne Masters   Client: Time-Life Records

85   Artist: **STEVE KARCHIN**   Art Director: Anne Masters   Client: Time-Life Records

86 Artist: **JOHN SCHOENHERR** Art Director: Rodney Williams Magazine: Science 81

87 Artist: **BERNIE FUCHS**   Art Director: Richard Gangel   Magazine: Sports Illustrated

88
Artist: **DAVID WILCOX**
Art Director: Jerry Alten
Magazine: TV Guide

89
Artist: **MICHAEL DUDASH**
Art Director: Tina Adamek
Magazine: The Physician &
Sportsmedicine

90
Artist: **SUE LLEWELLYN**
Art Director: James Smith
Magazine: Westward

91   Artist: **BILL DULA**   Art Director: Sheldon Hofmann   Client: NBC

92
Artist: **JIM WHITE**
Client: White-Eagle, Ltd

93 Artist: **CHRISTOPHER F. PAYNE**   Art Director: James Noel Smith   Magazine: Westward

94 Artist: **RICHARD SPARKS**   Art Director: Jerry Alten   Magazine: T.V. Guide

95 Artist: **DICK LUBEY** Art Director: David Boss Client: NFL Properties, Inc.

96 Artist: **HARRIET PERTCHIK**

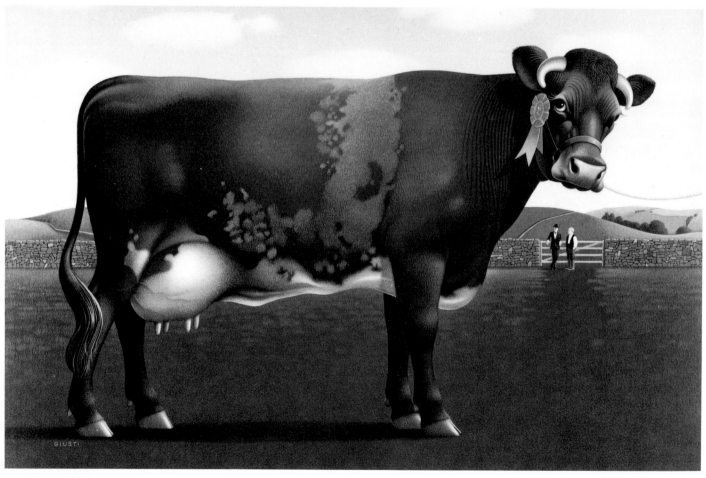

97 Artist: **ROBERT GIUSTI**   Art Director: Alvin Grossman   Magazine: McCall's

98
Artist: **DOUG KNUTSON**

99 Artist: **MARK ENGLISH**   Art Director: Sal Barracca   Magazine: Ladies' Home Journal

100 Artist: **ROBERT McGINNIS**   Art Director: Robert McGinnis   Client: Wayne Enterprises   **SILVER MEDAL**

101 Artist: **TOM ALLEN**   Art Director: Richard Gangel   Magazine: Sports Illustrated

102 Artist: **ROBERT McGINNIS**   Art Director: Robert McGinnis   Client: Husberg Galleries

103
Artist: **RICHARD SPARKS**
Art Director: Joe Connolly
Magazine: Boys' Life

104 Artist: **SKIP LIEPKE**

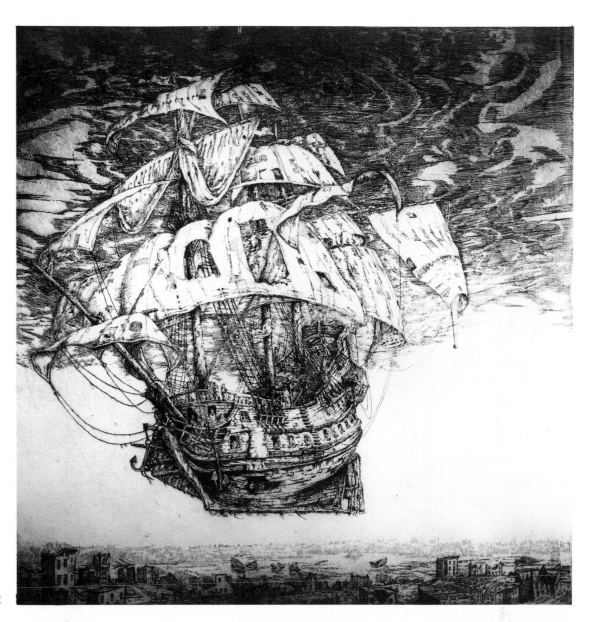

105
Artist: **MARK WHITCOMBE**

106
Artist: **WALTER HORTENS**

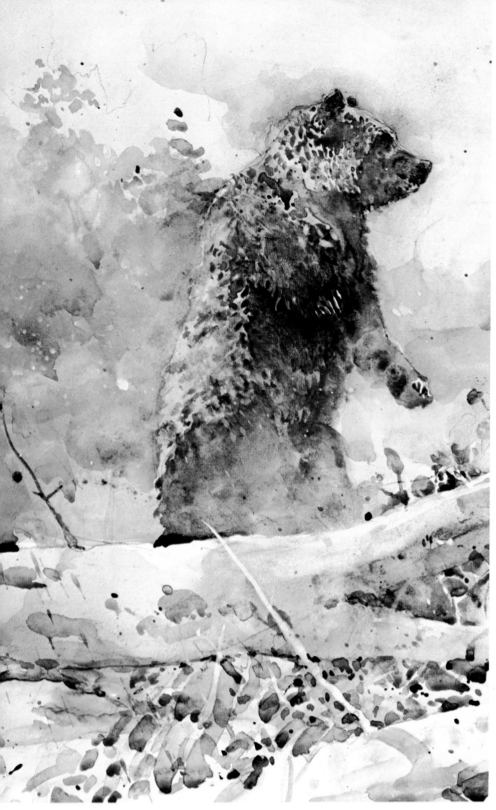

107
Artist: **CHARLES REID**
Art Director: Gary Gretter
Magazine: Sports Afield

108
Artist: **BARRON STOREY**
Art Director: Joe Connolly
Magazine: Boys' Life

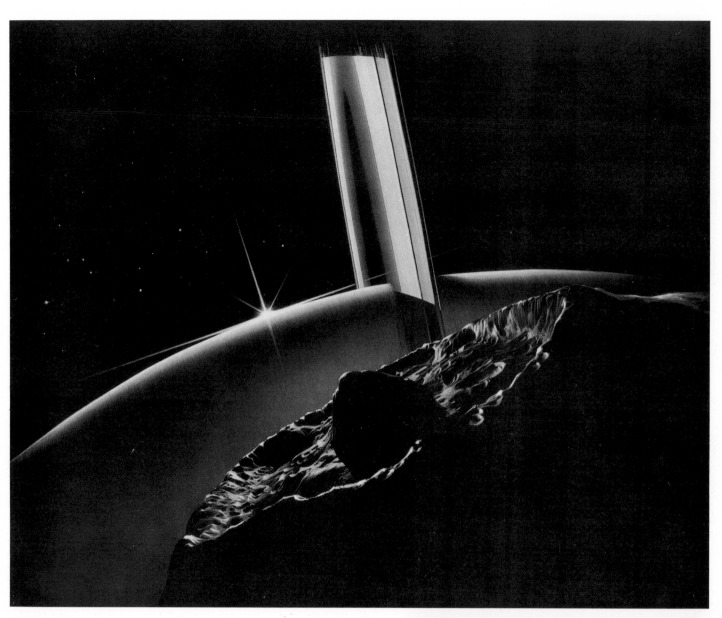

109
Artist: **WILLIAM H. BOND**
Art Director: Jan Adkins
Magazine: National Geographic

110
Artist: **ANDREA BARUFFI**
Art Director: Jeffrey Saks
Magazine: Art Direction

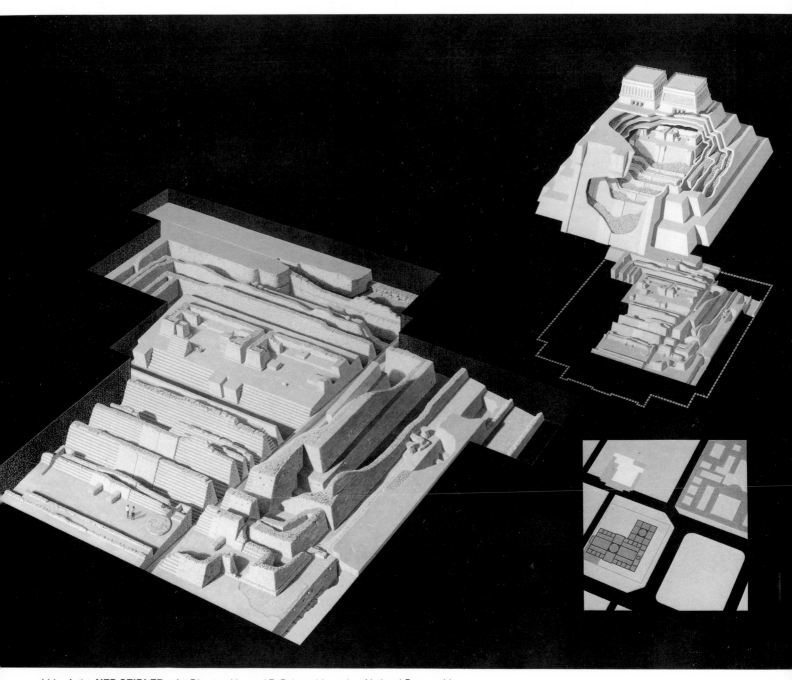

111 Artist: **NED SEIDLER** Art Director: Howard E. Paine Magazine: National Geographic

113
Artist: **BRAD HOLLAND**
Art Director: Jim Minnich
Client: Playboy Fashion Guide
SILVER MEDAL

112
Artist: **WILSON McLEAN**
Art Director: Joe Brooks
Magazine: Penthouse

BOOK

114
Artist: **DARRELL SWEET**
Art Director: Donald E. Munson
Client: Ballantine Books

115
Artist: **BERNIE FUCHS**
Art Directors: Jack Tauss/JoAnn Giaquinto
Publisher: The Franklin Library

SILVER MEDAL

116
Artist: **LINDA CROCKETT-HANZEL**
Art Director: Linda Crockett-Hanzel
Client: Bologna Children's Book Fair

GOLD MEDAL

117 Artist: **MAX GINSBURG**   Art Directors: Len Leone/Laura Glazer   Publisher: Bantam Books, Inc.

118 Artist: **BOB DAVIS**

119
Artist: **TOM FEELINGS**
Art Director: Atha Tehon
Publisher: The Dial Press

120   Artist: **ROBERT ANDREW PARKER**   Art Directors: Fabio Cohen/Frances Foster   Publisher: Knopf/Pantheon

121
Artist: **FREDERICKA RIBES**
Art Director: Milton Charles
Client: Pocket Books

122
Artist: **BERNIE FUCHS**
Art Director: William Gregory
Publisher: Reader's Digest

123 Artist: **JUDY PEDERSEN**

124 Artist: **ELLYN SIEGEL**

125
Artist: **STAN SKARDINSKI**
Art Director: Frank Kozelek
Publisher: Berkley Books

126   Artist: **RAPHAEL SOYER**   Art Director: Diana Klemin   Publisher: Doubleday & Co., Inc.

127 Artist: **MITCHELL HOOKS**   Art Director: Soren Noring   Publisher: Reader's Digest

128 Artist: **STEPHEN DE SANTO**   **SILVER MEDAL**

129
Artist: **STAN HUNTER**
Art Director: William Gregory
Publisher: Reader's Digest
SILVER MEDAL

130
Artist: **STAN HUNTER**
Art Director: William Gregory
Client: Reader's Digest

131
Artist: **VICTOR LAZZARO**
Art Director: Sheldon Cotler
Client: Time-Life Books

132 Artist: **DENNIS LUZAK**

133 Artist: **VICTOR LAZZARO**   Art Director: Sheldon Cotler   Client: Time-Life Books

134 Artist: **DAVID BLOSSOM**   Art Directors: Jody Bolt/Cinda Rose   Publisher: National Geographic Special Publications

THE BOOK OF
EBENEZER LE PAGE
a novel by G. B. Edwards

with an introduction by John Fowles

135 Artist: **DANIEL MAFFIA**   Art Director: Lidia Ferrara   Publisher: Alfred A. Knopf, Inc.   **SILVER MEDAL**

136
Artist: **BOB LAPSLEY**
Art Director: James Plumeri
Publisher: New American Library

137
Artist: **JAMES McMULLAN**
Art Director: James McMullan
Publisher: Watson-Guptill
SILVER MEDAL

138
Artist: **ROBERT G. STEELE**
Art Director: Chris Werner
Publisher: Harcourt Brace Jovanovich

139   Artist: **JERRY PINKNEY**   Art Director: Atha Tehon   Publisher: The Dial Press

140 Artist: **RICHARD CLIFF**

141 Artist: **RICK McCOLLUM**   Art Director: William Gregory   Publisher: Reader's Digest

142 Artist: **WENDELL MINOR**   Art Director: Robert Reed   Publisher: Holt, Rinehart & Winston

143
Artist: **LOU GLANZMAN**
Art Director: Len Leone
Publisher: Bantam Books, Inc.

144
Artist: **RICK McCOLLUM**
Art Director: William Gregory
Publisher: Reader's Digest

145
Artist: **MURRAY TINKELMAN**
Art Director: Milt Charles
Publisher: Pocket Books

146 Artist: **MURRAY TINKELMAN**

147 Artist: **MURRAY TINKELMAN**

148 Artist: **JACK ENDEWELT**

149
Artist: **JOHN M. THOMPSON**
Art Director: Len Leone
Publisher: Bantam Books, Inc.

150 Artist: **JOHN M. THOMPSON** Art Director: William Gregory Publisher: Reader's Digest

151 Artist: **DOUG CUSHMAN**

152 Artist: **JIM BEAUDOIN**

153   Artist: **JOHN M. KILROY**

154   Artist: **MARCIA BUJOLD**

155 Artist: **TONY CHEN**   Art Director: Anne Beneduce   Client: UNICEF

156
Artist: **TONY CHEN**
Art Director: Anne Beneduce
Client: UNICEF

157 Artist: **CHRISTOPHER BLOSSOM**   Art Director: Len Leone   Publisher: Bantam Books, Inc.

158 Artist: **CHRISTOPHER BLOSSOM** Art Director: Len Leone Publisher: Bantam Books, Inc.

159
Artist: **GIANNI BENVENUTI**
Art Director: Lee Fishback
Publisher: Berkley-Jove

160 Artist: **SUSAN JEFFERS**   Art Director: Atha Tehon   Publisher: The Dial Press

161 Artist: **MICHAEL BERENSTAIN**   Art Director: Cathy L. Goldsmith   Publisher: Random House, Inc.

162 Artist: **LOU GLANZMAN**   Art Director: Len Leone   Publisher: Bantam Books, Inc.

163 Artist: **PAUL O. ZELINSKY**   Art Director: Linn Fischer   Publisher: Knopf/Pantheon

164
Artist: **TED LEWIN**
Art Director: Soren Noring
Publisher: Reader's Digest

165   Artist: **JOHN M. THOMPSON**   Art Director: Donald E. Munson   Publisher: Ballantine Books

166
Artist: **GORDON JOHNSON**
Art Director: Barbara Bertoli
Publisher: Avon Books

167
Artist: **DON DAILY**
Art Director: Ed Rofheart
Client: Popular Library

168
Artist: **DARRELL SWEET**
Art Director: Donald E. Munson
Client: Ballantine Books

169 Artist: **DON IVAN PUNCHATZ** Art Directors: Frank Kozelek/Jim Lebbad Publisher: Berkley Books

170
Artist: **LLOYD BLOOM**
Art Director: Joy Chu
Publisher: Holt, Rinehart & Winston

171   Artist: **DAVID BLOSSOM**   Art Directors: Jody Bolt/Cinda Rose   Publisher: National Geographic Special Publications

172 Artist: **EDWARD SOREL**   Art Director: Cathy L. Goldsmith   Publisher: Random House

173 Artist: **EDWARD SOREL**   Art Director: Cathy L. Goldsmith   Publisher: Random House

174 Artist: **EDWARD SOREL** Art Director: Cathy L. Goldsmith Publisher: Random House

175 Artist: **HERBERT TAUSS**   Art Director: George Cornell   Publisher: Fawcett Books Group/A Division of CBS

176
Artist: **ANN MEISEL**
Art Director: Brad Benedict
Publisher: Harmony Books

177
Artist: **FRED PFEIFFER**
Art Director: Gerald Counihan
Publisher: Fawcett Books Group/A Division of CBS

178
Artist: **NEIL WALDMAN**
Art Directors: Bob Verrone/Dick Jackson
Publisher: Bradbury Press

179
Artist: **LOU GLANZMAN**
Art Director: Len Leone
Publisher: Bantam Books, Inc.

180 Artist: **STEVEN ASSEL**   Art Director: Barbara G. Hennessey   Publisher: Viking Penguin, Inc.

181 Artist: **ROBERT G. STEELE**

182 Artist: **PETER McCAFFREY**

183　Artist: **ROBERT G. STEELE**

184　Artist: **JOHN WHALLEY**

185
Artists: **LEO & DIANE DILLON**
Art Director: Barbara Bertoli
Publisher: Avon Books

186
Artist: **RICK McCOLLUM**
Art Director: William Gregory
Publisher: Reader's Digest

187
Artist: **HERBERT TAUSS**
Art Director: Barbara Bertoli
Publisher: Avon Books

188 Artist: **EZRA N. TUCKER** Art Director: Nancy Krause

189   Artist: **SUSAN WELT**

190   Artist: **SUSAN WELT**

191 Artist: **JOYCE JOHN**

192
Artist: **JOHN CAMEJO**
Art Director: Grey Williams
Publisher: Communications Publications

193 Artist: **HEIDI HOLDER** Art Director: Barbara G. Hennessy Publisher: Viking Penguin Inc.

194
Artist: **JOHN O'BRIEN**
Art Director: Evelyne Johnson
Client: Sharon Publishing

195   Artist: **HEIDI HOLDER**   Art Director: Barbara G. Hennessy   Publisher: Viking Penguin Inc.

196
Artist: **LLOYD BLOOM**
Art Director: Joy Chu
Publisher: Holt, Rinehart & Winston

197
Artist: **JOANNE L. SCRIBNER**
Art Director: Bruce Hall
Publisher: Dell Publishing

198
Artist: **MICHAEL GARLAND**
Art Director: Jean Karl
Client: Atheneum

199   Artist: **NEIL FEIGELES**

200 Artist: **ANGELA WERNEKE** Art Director: Peter Aschwanden Publisher: John Muir Publications

And then we say goodnight.

BCDEFGHIJ

201   Artist: **ELOISE WILKIN**   Art Director: Grace Clarke   Publisher: Golden Books, Western Publishing

202 Artist: **KRISTINA RODANAS**

203
Artist: **JOANNE L. SCRIBNER**
Art Director: Bruce Hall
Publisher: Dell Publishing

204
Artist: **KRISTINA RODANAS**
Art Director: Mary Jane Dunton
Publisher: Scholastic, Inc.

205
Artist: **LLOYD BLOOM**
Art Director: Betty Anderson
Publisher: Alfred A. Knopf, Inc.

206 Artist: **ERIC VINCENT**

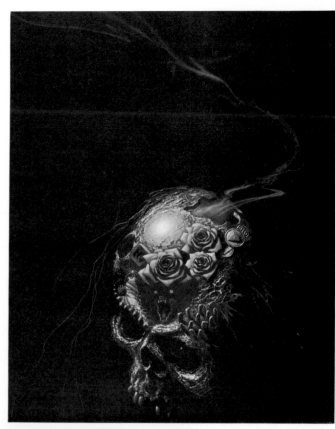

207   Artist: **MICHAEL WHELAN**

208   Artist: **JOHN BERKEY**

209 Artist: **SAUL MANDEL**

210 Artist: **ALEX O'NEAL**

211 Artist: **TOMIE dePAOLA** Art Director: Kay Jerman Publisher: Holiday House, Inc.

212
Artist: **KINUKO Y. CRAFT**
Art Director: Barbara Bertoli
Publisher: Bard/Avon Books

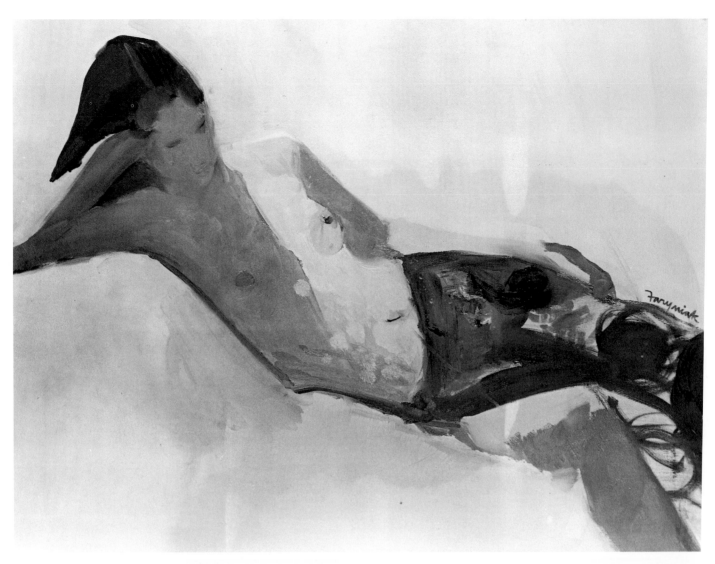

213 Artist: **KAREN FARYNIAK**

214 Artist: **BILL JOYNER**

215 Artist: **KAREN FARYNIAK**

216 Artist: **MALOU FLATO**

217
Artist: **BOB DACEY**
Art Director: Jack Tauss
Publisher: The Franklin Library

218
Artist: **MICHAEL WHELAN**
Art Director: Charles Volpe
Publisher: Ace Books

219 Artist: **LEONARD BASKIN** Art Director: Barbara G. Hennessy Publisher: Viking Penguin, Inc.

220
Artist: **JIM SPANFELLER**
Art Director: Jack Tauss
Publisher: The Franklin Library

221　Artist: **DON McROBERT**

222 Artist: **MARILYN MARK**

223 Artist: **JIM BEAUDOIN**

224 Artist: **ROLAND DESCOMBES**

225 Artist: **STAN GALLI**   Art Director: William Gregory   Publisher: Reader's Digest

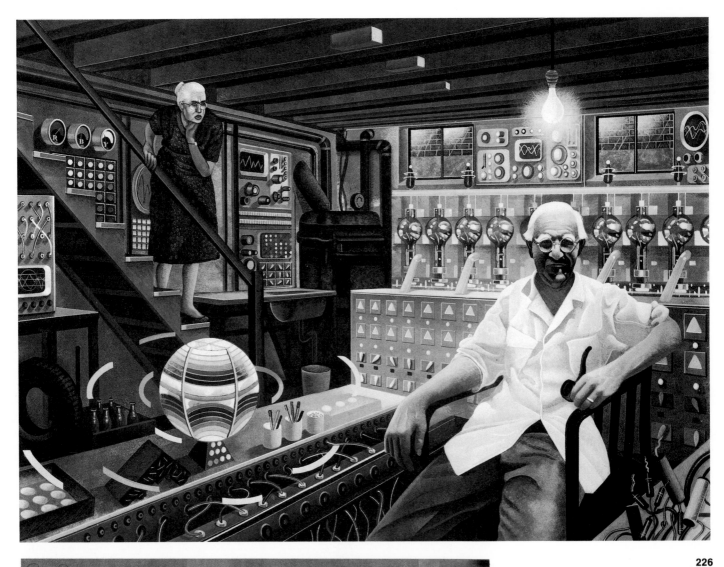

226
Artist: **TOM LEONARD**
Art Director: Brian Cody
Publisher: Raintree Publishers Group

227 Artist: **CAROL WALD**

228
Artist: **DAVID GROVE**
Art Director: Len Leone
Publisher: Bantam Books, Inc.

229   Artist: **TOM HALE**   Client: Automotive Fine Art

230
Artist: **GARY VISKUPIC**
Art Director: Francis Tanabe
Client: Washington Post (Book World)

231
Artist: **JIM WHITE**
Client: White-Eagle, Ltd

232
Artist: **DENNIS LYALL**
Art Director: Richard Carter
Publisher: Easton Press

233   Artist: **KAREN FARYNIAK**

234
Artist: **HERBERT TAUSS**
Art Director: Jack Tauss
Publisher: The Franklin Library

235
Artist: **BRUCE WALDMAN**
Art Director: Neil Stuart
Publisher: Penguin Books

236 Artist: **MITCHELL HOOKS**   Art Director: Jack Tauss   Publisher: The Franklin Library

237 Artist: **ROBERT J. LEE**   Art Directors: John Witt/Cathy deMartin   Agency: Ruvane-Leverte   Client: Astra Pharmaceuticals

238 Artist: **RICHARD SPARKS** Art Director: Richard Carter Publisher: Easton Press

239
Artist: **SANDY KOSSIN**
Art Director: Gerald Counihan
Publisher: Fawcett Book Group/A Division of CBS

240 Artist: **RON LIZORTY**

241 Artist: **MITCHELL HOOKS** Art Director: Soren Noring Publisher: Reader's Digest

242
Artist: **BEN WOHLBERG**
Art Director: Soren Noring
Publisher: Reader's Digest

243
Artist: **TOM HALL**
Art Director: Donald E. Munson
Publisher: Ballantine Books

244 Artist: **JAMES McMULLAN**   Art Director: James McMullan   Publisher: Watson-Guptill

245 Artist: **STEPHEN DE SANTO**

246
Artist: **JEAN CARLSON MASSEAU**

247 Artist: **LOU MYERS** Art Director: Paul Hanson Publisher: Workman Publishing

248
Artist: **JOHN BERKEY**
Art Director: Len Leone
Publisher: Bantam Books, Inc.

249
Artist: **CHRISTOPHER BLOSSOM**
Art Director: Len Leone
Publisher: Bantam Books, Inc.

JURORS

GORDON JOHNSON, Chairman
Freelance illustrator specializing
in paperback cover art.

RON CAMPBELL
Art Director, Fortune Magazine.
Awards from Society of Illustrators,
American Institute of Graphic Arts,
Art Direction and Communication Arts.

DIANE DILLON
Freelance illustrator with partner Leo Dillon.
National President, Graphic Artists Guild.
Treasurer, Society of Illustrators, 1980-82.
Won Society's Hamilton King Award and
American Library Association's Caldecott Award.

DONALD DUFFY
Corporate Art Director, Reader's Digest.

NED GLATTAUER
Freelance illustrator.
Treasurer, Society of Illustrators.

SIMMS TABACK
Freelance illustrator.
Faculty, School of Visual Arts.
President, Graphic Artists Guild, NY.
Past President, Illustrators Guild.
Exhibited at Society of Illustrators,
Art Directors Club,
American Institute of Graphic Arts.

JOHN THOMPSON
Freelance illustrator.

BOB DACEY
Freelance illustrator.
Faculty, Sacred Heart University.
Society of Illustrators Annual
Exhibition award winner.

ADVERTISING

250 Artist: **JAMES McMULLAN** Art Director: Steve Sessions Agency: Baxter & Korge, Inc. Client: Four-Leaf Towers

251
Artist: **DANIEL SCHWARTZ**
Art Director: Ivan Chermayeff
Client: Mobil
GOLD MEDAL

252   Artist: **KUNIO HAGIO**   Art Director: Marcos Kemp   Agency: N.W. Ayer ABH International   Client: ABC-WLS TV   **SILVER MEDAL**

253   Artist: **BURT SILVERMAN**   Art Director: Ivan Chermayeff   Client: Mobil

255
Artist: **BOB PEAK**
Art Director: Don Smolen
Agency: Smolen, Smith & Connolly
Client: Zoetrope Productions

254
Artist: **BOB PEAK**
Art Director: Don Smolen
Agency: Smolen, Smith & Connolly
Client: Orion
GOLD MEDAL

257 Artist: **DON DAILY** Art Director: Joan Barron Agency: BBD&O Client: Hammermill Paper Company

258
Artist: **BOB ZIERING**
Art Director: Kevin Kearns
Agency: Mullen Advertising
Client: Trak Skis

259
Artist: **KATHERYN HOLT**
Art Director: Pat McGowan
Client: RCA Records

260
Artists: **LEO & DIANE DILLON**
Art Director: Michael Goode
Client: Caedmon Records

261
Artist: **NORMAN WALKER**
Art Directors: Bill Levy/Bob Heimall
Client: Polygram Records
SILVER MEDAL

FEAR

OF THE UNKNOWN

262
Artists: **GRIESBACH/MARTUCCI**
Art Director: Alan Davis
Client: London Records

263
Artist: **DANIEL MAFFIA**
Art Director: Ron Kellum
Client: RCA Records

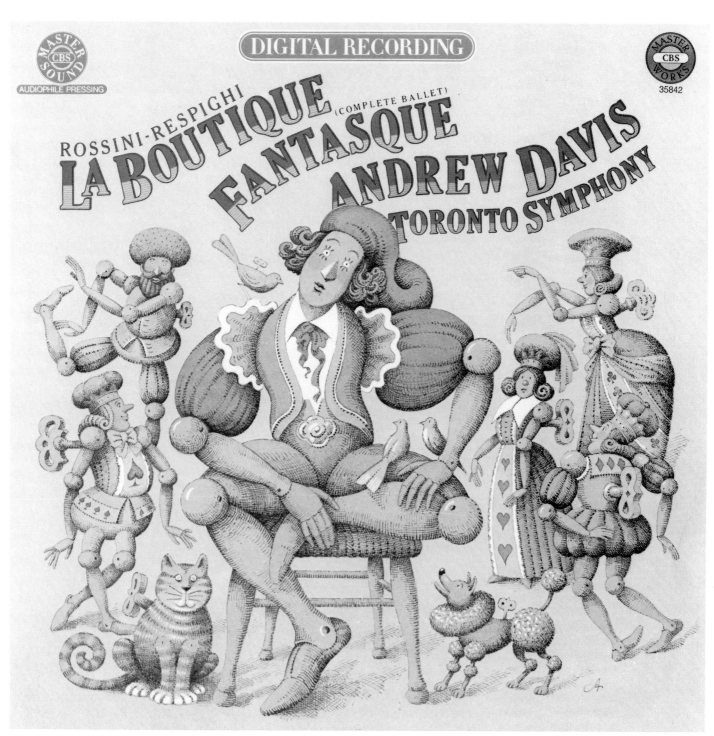

265
Artist: **GARY KELLEY**
Client: UNI Lyric Theatre
GOLD MEDAL

266   Artist: **MARK ENGLISH**   Art Director: Doug Fisher   Agency: Lord, Sullivan & Yoder   Client: Nevamar Corp.   **SILVER MEDAL**

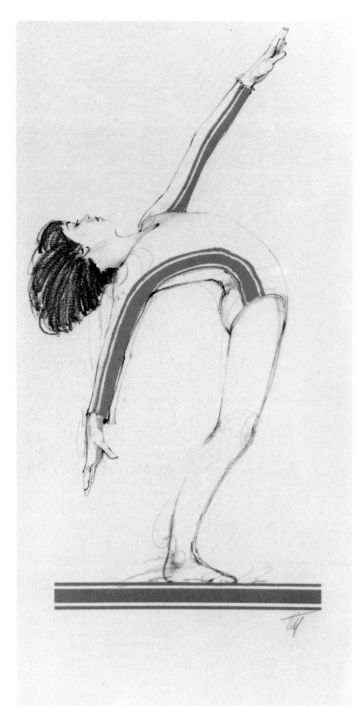

267
Artist: **TIM BRUCE**
Art Director: Edyce Hall
Client: R.J. Reynolds Industries, Inc.

268
Artist: **W.C. ERSLAND**
Client: Barbara Harbach

269
Artist: **WINIFRED GODFREY**
Art Director: William R. Sample
Client: Abbott Laboratories

270
Artist: **BOB PEAK**
Art Director: Larry Lurin
Agency: Rosebud Advertising Corp.
Client: MGM

271 Artist: **CAROL WALD**   Art Director: Tom Null   Client: Varese Sarabande Records, Inc.

273
Artist: **ELIZABETH F. BENNETT**
Art Director: Joseph Stelmach
Client: RCA Records

274 Artists: **BILL STEPHENS/RON SAUTER** Client: Red Creek Inn

275 Artist: **DENNIS LUZAK**

276
Artist: **MARIO A. ROSETTI**
Art Director: Mario A. Rosetti
Client: Robert Andersen

278　Artist: **JERRY HARSTON**　Art Director: Greg Wilder

277
Artist: **RICHARD SPARKS**
Art Director: Joseph Stelmach
Client: RCA Records

279 Artist: **PAMELA HIGGINS**

280
Artist: **IVAN POWELL**
Art Director: Debra Hovhannisian
Agency: BBD&O
Client: Hammermill Papers Group

281
Artist: **CHARLES SANTORE**
Art Directors: Susan Lyster/Peggy Petos
Agency: McCaffrey & McCall
Client: N.E.T./Exxon

282
Artist: **JOHN COLLIER**
Art Director: Paula Scher
Client: CBS Records

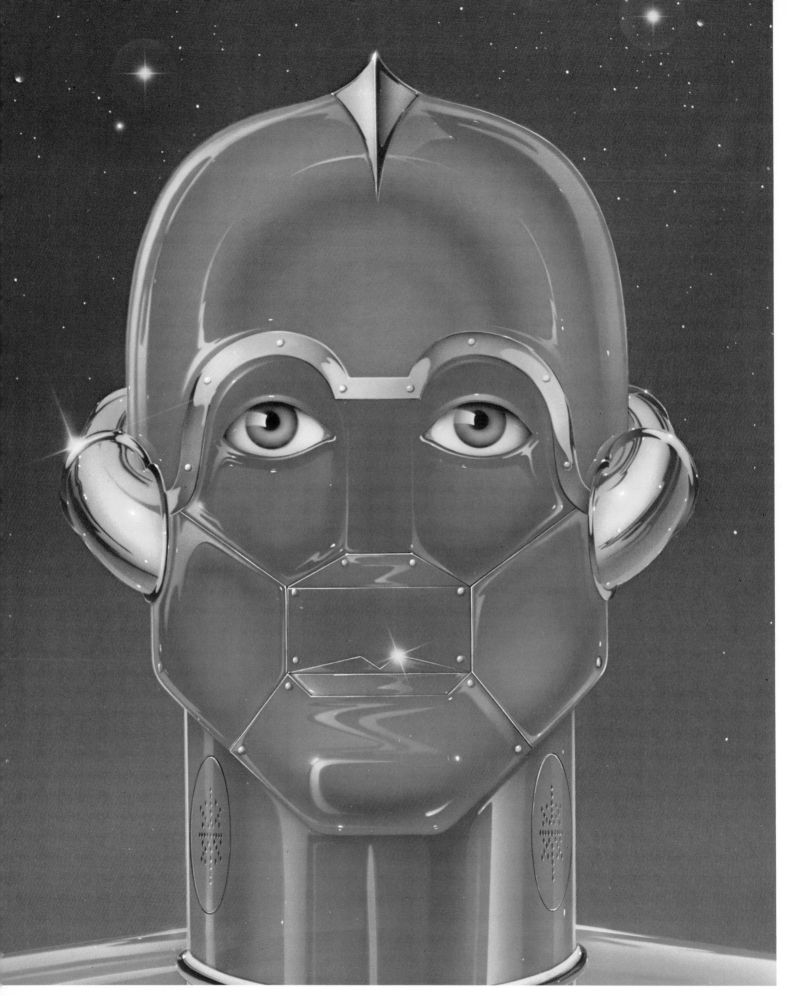

283 Artist: **DICKRAN PALULIAN** · Art Director: Paul Regan · Agency: HHCC · Client: N.E.C.

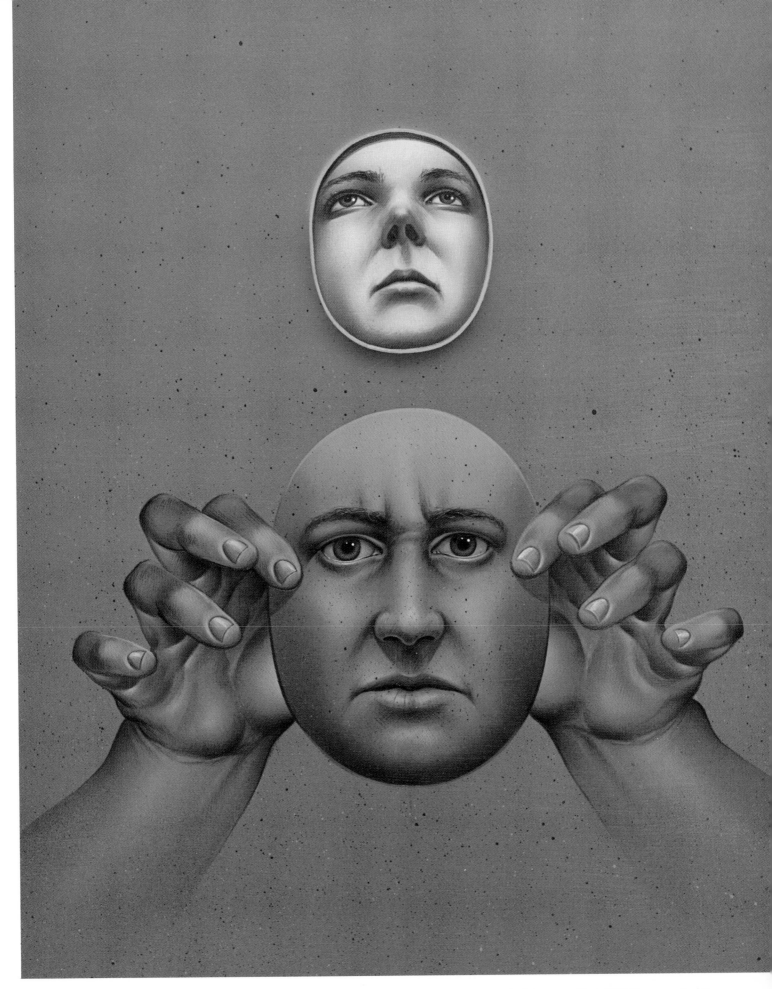

284   Artist: **PAUL STINSON**   Art Director: John Kashiwabara   Agency: C&G Agency   Client: CIBA Pharmaceutical Co.

285
Artist: **JOHN BERKEY**
Art Director: Seymon Ostilly
Agency: Lord, Geller, Federico, Einstein, Inc.
Client: IBM

286 Artists: **GRIESBACH/MARTUCCI**

287 Artist: **JIM SPANFELLER**   Art Director: Blaine Gutermuth   Agency: Howard Swink, Inc.   Client: Owens-Illinois

288
Artist: **BRUCE WOLFE**
Art Director: Dennis Ivan
Agency: Grey Advertising
Client: San Miguel International

289   Artist: **SUSAN SUMICHRAST**

290
Artist: **BRUCE WOLFE**
Art Director: Dennis Ivan
Agency: Grey Advertising
Client: San Miguel International

291   Artist: **WILSON McLEAN**   Art Director: Len Sirowitz   Agency: Rosenfeld, Sirowitz & Lawson, Inc.   Client: Champion International

292 Artist: **JOHN M. THOMPSON**   Art Director: Bob Reedy   Agency: Needham, Harper & Steers   Client: Busch Beer

293
Artist: **DOUG JOHNSON**
Art Director: John Wilner
Agency: Ash Ledonne
Client: Onward Victoria

294
Artist: **JEFF WACK**
Art Director: Bill Burks
Client: United Artists Records

295 Artist: **BUD KEMPER**   Agency: Maritz Motivation   Client: Anheuser-Busch

296
Artist: **TOM CURRY**
Art Director: Tom Curry
Client: Clampitt Paper Co.

297   Artist: **CHARLES SANTORE**   Art Director: David Bartels   Agency: The Hanley Partnership   Client: Busch Beer

298
Artist: **BARNETT PLOTKIN**
Art Director: Bill Coyne
Client: Big Ben

299   Artist: **BURT SILVERMAN**   Art Director: Seymon Ostilly   Agency: Lord, Geller, Frederico, Einstein, Inc.   Client: IBM

300
Artist: **DOUG JOHNSON**
Art Director: Gayl Ware
Agency: Rives, Smith, Baldwin & Carlberg
Client: Gulf Oil

301
Artist: **MAURICE LEWIS**
Art Director: Cliff Gillock
Agency: First Marketing Group
Client: First NBC

302 Artist: **FRED OTNES**   Art Director: Vince Maiello   Client: Playboy Book Club

303   Artist: **WENDELL MINOR**   Art Director: Atha Tehon   Publisher: The Dial Press

304 Artist: **BOB ZIERING** Art Directors: Rene Disbrow/Olaf Moetus Agency: Foote, Cone & Belding Client: First National Bank of Chicago

305 Artist: **CHARLES LILLY** Art Director: Frank Barrows Agency: Young & Rubicam Client: UNCF

306 Artist: **KENNETH FRANCIS DEWEY**

307 Artist: **BRUCE EMMETT**   Art Director: Steve Parenti   Agency: Kurtz & Tarlow Co.   Client: Ralph Lauren — Chaps

308
Artist: **ROBERT HEINDEL**
Art Directors: Robert Paige/Richard Loomis
Agency: Evans Garber & Paige, Inc.
Client: Duofold, Inc.

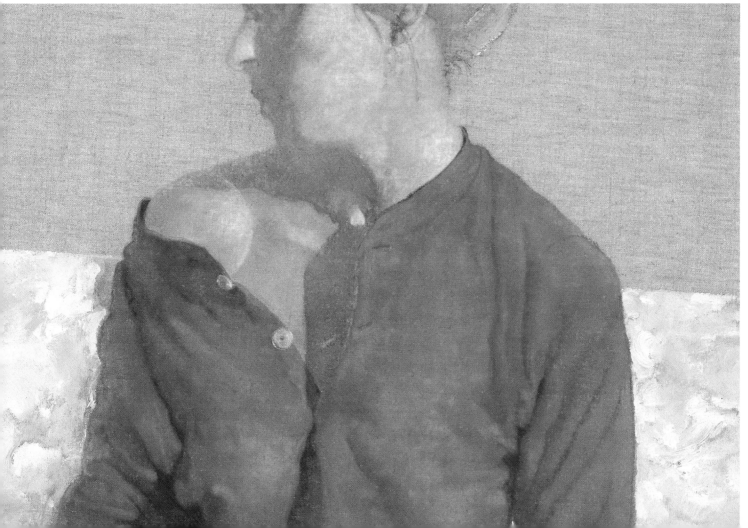

309
Artist: **GERRY GERSTEN**
Art Director: Philip Growick
Agency: Philip Growick Assoc.
Client: Industrial Education

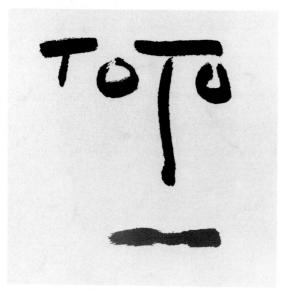

310
Artist: **TONY LANE**
Art Director: Tony Lane
Client: CBS Records

311
Artist: **JEFF SEAVER**
Art Director: Jeff Seaver
Client: Graphic Artists Guild

312
Artist: **CHARLES WELLS**
Art Director: Joseph Stelmach
Client: RCA Records

313
Artist: **JACK PARDUE**
Art Director: Jack Pardue
Client: KX Country Radio

314
Artist: **CATHERINE HUERTA**
Art Director: Catherine Huerta   Client: Bernstein & Andriulli

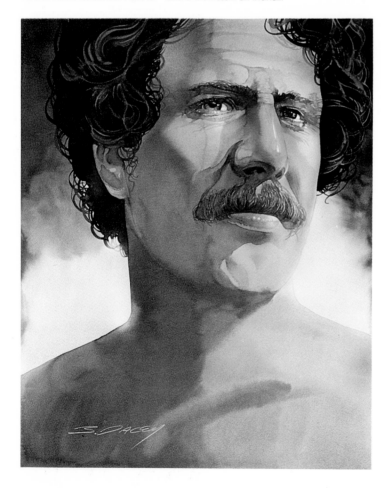

315
Artist: **BOB DACEY**
Art Director: Vince Maiello
Client: Playboy Book Club

316 Artist: **ALLEN WELKIS** Art Director: Russ Patrick Client: Sony

317 Artist: **DAVE BECK**

318
Artist: **AL PISANO**
Art Director: Anne Masters
Client: Time-Life Records

319
Artist: **JACK de GRAFFENRIED**
Art Director: Dolores Gudzin
Client: NBC

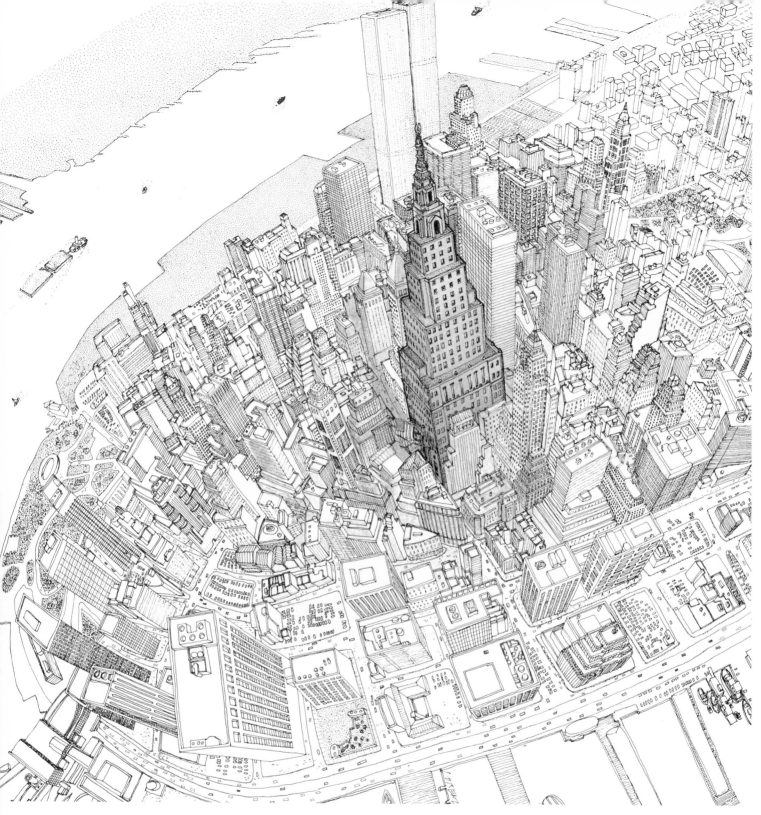

320
Artist: **AL LORENZ**
Art Director: John Garre
Agency: Doremus Advertising
Client: Bank of New York

321
Artist: **WALTER FRANK BOMAR**
Art Director: Cathy Bley
Agency: Young & Rubicam, Inc.
Client: Eastern Airlines

322
Artist: **GARY MEYER**
Art Director: Tom Tieche
Agency: Ogilvy & Mather, Inc.
Client: Blitz Weinhard Co.

323
Artist: **MARGARET CUSACK**
Art Director: Ruth Brody
Client: B. Altman's & Co.

324 Artist: **JOHN BERKEY**

325
Artist: **ROBERT GIUSTI**
Art Director: Sandi Young
Client: Atlantic Records

326 Artist: **ARTHUR SHILSTONE** Art Director: Robert Schulman Client: NASA

327
Artist: **BRETT SMITH**
Art Director: Mike Thoth
Client: Wembley Industries

328
Artist: **JEFF WACK**
Art Director: Henry Vizcarra
Client: Warner, Elektra, Atlantic

329
Artist: **BERNIE FUCHS**
Art Director: Jack O'Grady
Client: Jack O'Grady

330
Artist: **WINSLOW PINNEY PELS**
Art Director: Winslow Pinney Pels
Agency: Madison North
Client: Empire State Youth Theatre

331
Artist: **JERRY PINKNEY**
Art Directors: Dave Foot/Ken Fay
Client: U.S. Postal Service

332
Artist: **GERRY GERSTEN**
Art Director: Joel Fuller
Agency: Mike Sloan Inc.
Client: Ryder Trucks

333
Artist: **BRUCE WOLFE**
Art Director: Dennis Ivan
Agency: Grey Advertising
Client: San Miguel International

334 Artist: **ELLEN RIXFORD**   Art Director: John Fraioli   Agency: Bergelt Advertising   Client: Schering

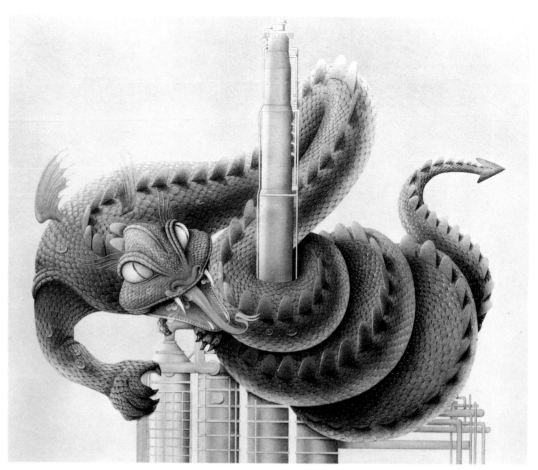

336
Artist: **LINDA GIST**
Art Directors: Jack Taylor/Elmer Pizzi
Agency: Gray & Rogers, Inc.
Art Director: Diamond Shamrock

337
Artist: **DON IVAN PUNCHATZ**
Art Director: Simon Bowden
Agency: Needam Harper & Steers
Client: Union Carbide

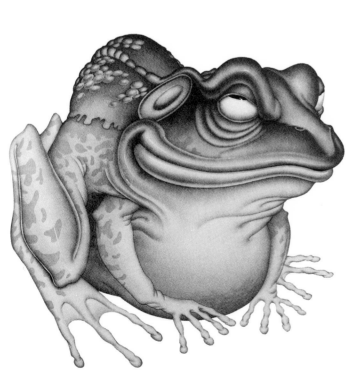

339
Artist: **BOB RADIGAN**
Art Director: Elmer Pizzi
Agency: Gray & Rogers, Inc.
Client: Grit

340
Artist: **MITCH HYATT**
Art Director: Elmer Pizzi
Agency: Gray & Rogers, Inc.
Client: Grit

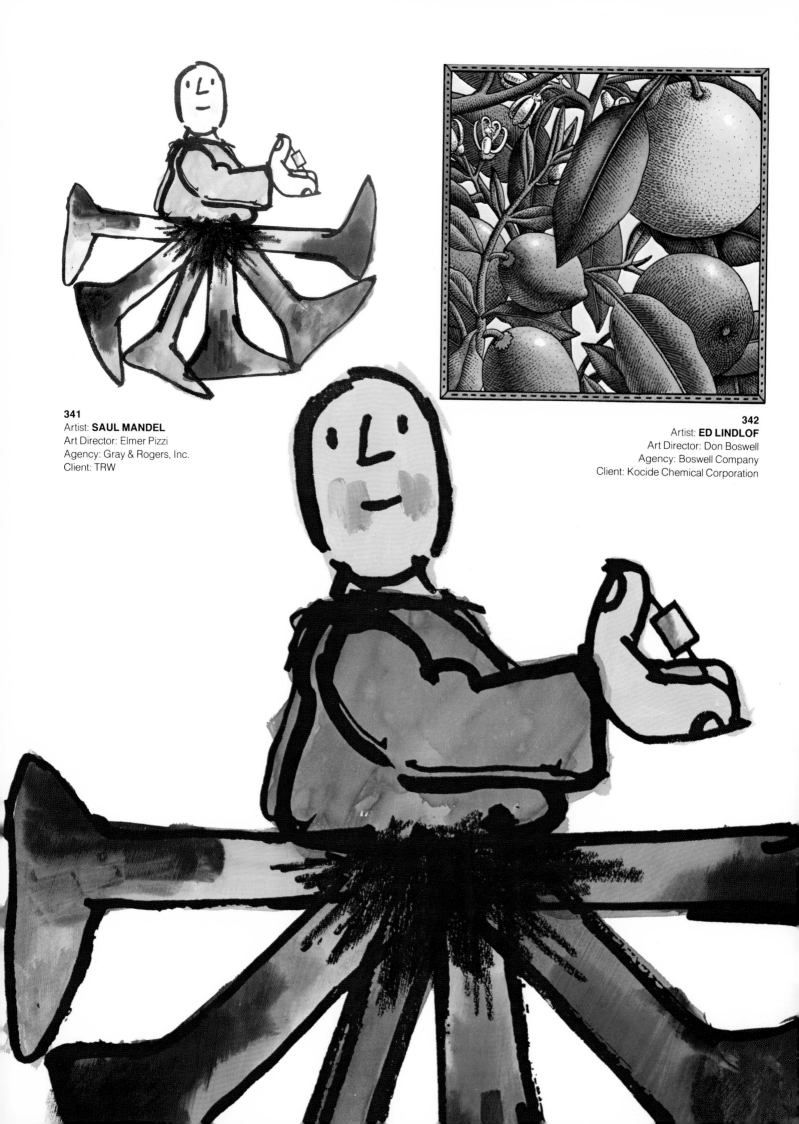

341
Artist: **SAUL MANDEL**
Art Director: Elmer Pizzi
Agency: Gray & Rogers, Inc.
Client: TRW

342
Artist: **ED LINDLOF**
Art Director: Don Boswell
Agency: Boswell Company
Client: Kocide Chemical Corporation

343 Artist: **SUSAN HUNT-WULKOWICZ**   Art Director: William R. Sample   Client: Abbott Laboratories

344 Artist: **JACK ENDEWELT**

345 Artist: **JACK UNRUH**   Art Director: Dick Moulton   Agency: Howard Swink, Inc.   Client: Owens-Illinois

346
Artist: **BEATRICE TAGGART**
Art Director: Arthur Kaufman
Agency: Lavey/Wolff/Swift, Inc.
Client: Ames Division, Miles Laboratories

347
Artist: **DON IVAN PUNCHATZ**
Art Director: Simon Bowden
Agency: Needam Harper & Steers
Client: Union Carbide

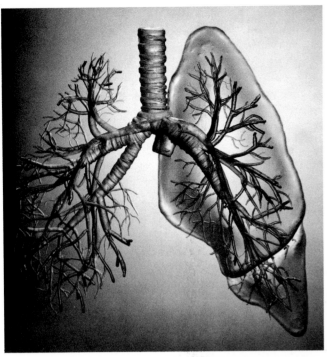

348
Artist: **KIRK MOLDOFF**
Art Directors: Neil Ferrara/Skip Hurley
Agency: M.E.D. Communications
Client: Squibb International

349
Artist: **WALT SPITZMILLER**
Art Director: James Dalthorp
Agency: McCann Erickson, Inc.
Client: Abercrombie & Fitch

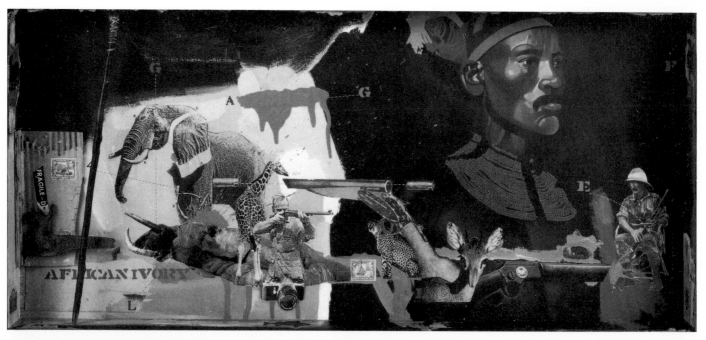

350 Artist: **STEVE KARCHIN** Art Director: Vince Maiello Client: Playboy Book Club

351 Artist: **DAVE BECK** Art Director: Bob Meyer Client: Jack O'Grady

352
Artist: **TOM BOOKWALTER**
Art Director: Tina Wilcox
Client: Josten's

353
Artist: **DOUG JOHNSON**
Art Director: Terry Watson
Agency: Gilmore Advertising

354
Artist: **DON WELLER**
Art Director: Carl Leick
Client: Western Airlines

355
Artist: **MILTON GLASER**
Art Director: Milton Glaser
Client: Saratoga Performing Arts Center

356
Artist: **DAVID KILMER**
Agency: R & R Advertising
Client: U.S. Senator Paul Laxalt

357
Artist: **ALFRED 'CHIEF' JOHNSON**
Art Director: Alfred 'Chief' Johnson
Client: Sanders Associates, Inc.

358
Artist: **FRANK SASO**

359
Artist: **LOUIS ESCOBEDO**
Art Director: Ron Martin
Client: Corps of Cadets —
Texas A&M University

360
Artist: **WALT SPITZMILLER**
Art Director: Don Komai
Client: Time-Life Records

361 Artist: **ALLEN J. BIANCHI** Art Director: Joseph Stelmach Client: RCA Records

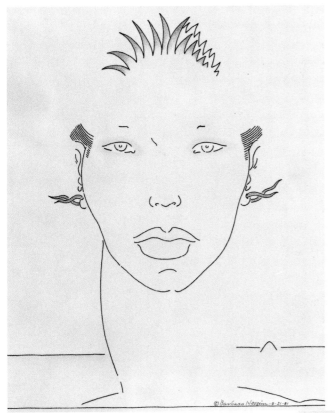

362
Artist: **BARBARA NESSIM**
Art Directors: Barbara Nessim/Mare Earley
Client: Scarlett Letters

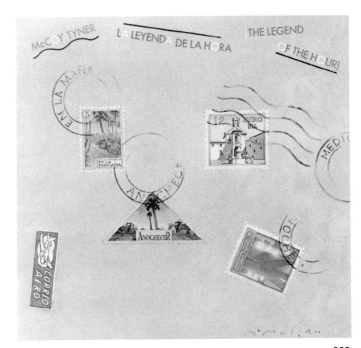

363
Artist: **JAMES McMULLAN**
Art Director: Carin Goldberg
Client: CBS Records

364
Artist: **THEA KLIROS**
Art Director: Ina Kahn
Client: Trevira

365
Artist: **BOB DACEY**
Art Director: John W. Channell
Client: Sony Corp. of America

366 Artist: **ROBERT HEINDEL**   Art Director: Vince Maiello   Client: Playboy Book Club

367
Artist: **JEFF PIENKOS**
Art Director: William R. Sample
Client: Abbott Laboratories

368   Artist: **BOB DACEY**   Art Director: Vince Maiello   Client: Playboy Book Club

369
Artist: **DENNIS LUZAK**
Art Directors: Acy R. Lehman/Dick Smith
Client: RCA SelectaVision

370
Artist: **WINSLOW PINNEY PELS**
Art Directors: Winslow Pinney Pels/Lynn Hollyn
Agency: Madison North
Client: Empire State Youth Theatre

ALICE CHILDRESS

Rainbow Jordan

by the author of A HERO AIN'T NOTHIN BUT A SANDWICH

ALICE CHILDRESS

Rainbow Jordan

COWARD, McCANN & GEOGHEGAN

371 Artist: **JERRY PINKNEY** Art Director: Catherine Stock Client: Coward, McCann & Geoghegan

372 Artist: **KIRSTEN SODERLIND** Art Director: Nick Giroffi Agency: William Douglas McAdams Client: Carter Wallace Inc.

373
Artist: **BARBARA NESSIM**
Art Director: Henrietta Condak
Client: CBS Records

374
Artist: **RICHARD KREPEL**
Art Directors: Acy R. Lehman/Dick Smith
Client: RCA SelectaVision

375
Artist: **DEBBIE KUHN**
Art Director: Frank Rizzo
Agency: Tracy-Locke
Client: Phillips Petroleum

376   Artist: **TRACY SABIN**   Art Director: Tracy Sabin   Client: Japanese Village Plaza

377 Artist: **DAGMAR FRINTA** Art Director: Christopher Austopchuk Client: CBS Records

378
Artist: **KUNIO HAGIO**
Art Director: Joe Minnella
Agency: W.B. Doner & Co.
Client: Michigan Chamber of Commerce

379 Artist: **JOHN LYTLE**   Art Director: Chris Shorten   Agency: D'Arcy-MacManus & Masius   Client: Bank of America

380   Artist: **DAVE BECK**

381
Artist: **CAROL WALD**
Art Director: Ron Kellum
Client: RCA Records

382
Artist: **ALAN REINGOLD**
Art Director: Sherry Pollack
Agency: McCaffrey & McCall
Client: Exxon/PBS

383
Artist: **GREG HARGREAVES**

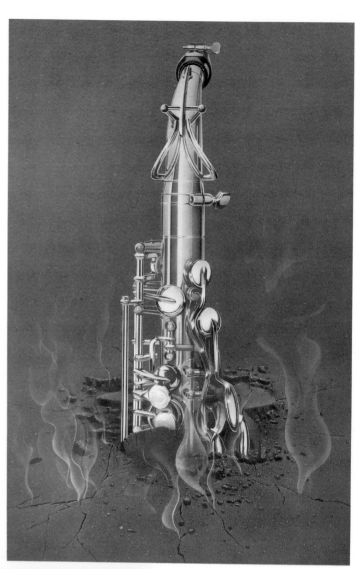

384
Artist: **DICKRAN PALULIAN**
Art Director: Steve Phillips
Client: Steve Phillips Design

385
Artist: **ROGER HUYSSEN**
Art Director: John Berg
Client: CBS Records

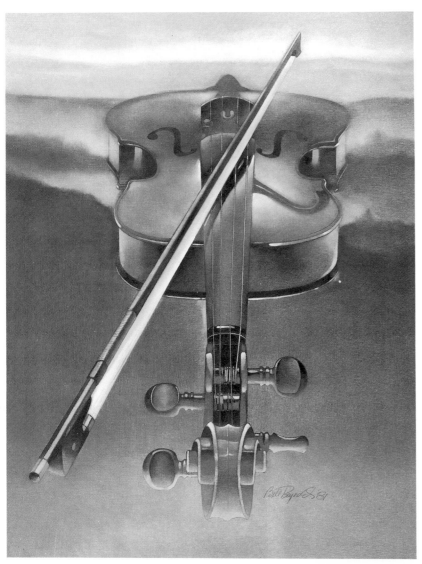

386
Artist: **WILLIAM G. REYNOLDS**
Art Director: Mark Warne
Client: Republic Airlines

387
Artist: **DAVID WILCOX**
Art Director: Allen Weinberg
Client: CBS Records

389
Artist: **JACK PARDUE**
Art Director: Anne Masters
Client: Time-Life Books

390 Artists: **BILL STEPHENS/RON SAUTER** Client: Red Creek Inn

388 Artist: **BART FORBES** Art Director: Jack O'Grady Client: Jack O'Grady

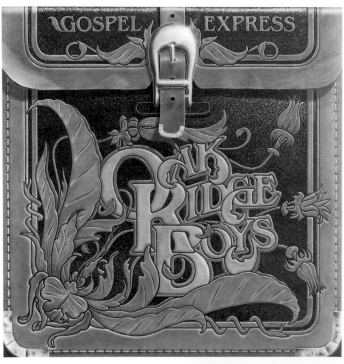

391
Artist: **TRACY W. BRITT**
Art Director: Bill Brunt
Client: Heartwarming Records

392
Artist: **BERNIE FUCHS**
Art Director: Susan Kennedy
Client: E.S.P.N.

393 Artist: **GREG HARGREAVES**

394
Artist: **ROBERT M. CUNNINGHAM**
Art Director: Terry Watson
Agency: Gilmore Advertising
Client: Upjohn

396
Artist: **DAN LONG**
Art Director: Tim Hallinan
Agency: Stone Associates
Client: PBS/Lutheren Brotherhood

395
Artist: **JERRY PINKNEY**
Art Director: Joseph Stelmach
Client: RCA Records

397   Artist: **JOHN GAMACHE**

JURORS

DENNIS LUZAK, Chairman
Freelance illustrator.
Awarded Jacques Gold Medal.

ROBERT O. BACH
Senior Vice-President, Creative Director, Mel Richman, Inc.
Past President, American Institute of Graphic Arts.

BETTY FRASER
Freelance illustrator specializing in flora and fauna
pen and ink drawings.
Secretary, Society of Illustrators.

SKIP LIEPKE
Freelance illustrator.
Won Society of Illustrators Annual Exhibition Past
Chairmen's Special Award in 1981 and 1982.

CHARLES McVICKER
Freelance illustrator. Past President, Society of Illustrators.

RON MEYERSON
Cover Art Director, Senior Editor, Newsweek Magazine.

DONALD MUNSON
Art Director, Ballantine, Fawcett & DelRey Books.

EILEEN HEDY SCHULTZ
Art Director, Good Housekeeping magazine.
Teaches at School of Visual Arts and Syracuse University.
Chairman, Joint Ethics Committee.
Past President, Art Directors Club.

INSTITUTIONAL

398
Artist: **JOHN ALCORN**
Art Director: Peter Rauch
Client: Young Presidents Organization
SILVER MEDAL

399
Artist: **JON McINTOSH**
Art Director: Jon McIntosh
Client: Boston Symphony Auction

400
Artist: **LONNI SUE JOHNSON**
Art Director: Peg Patterson
Client: The Producer

401 Artist: **WILSON McLEAN**   Art Director: Steve Miller   Agency: Garrison, Jasper & Rose, Inc.

402
Artist: **MIMI VANG OLSEN**
Art Director: Mimi Vang Olsen
Client: Smith Gallery

403
Artist: **MIMI VANG OLSEN**
Art Director: Mimi Vang Olsen
Client: Carolyn Bean Publishing

404   Artist: **ROBERT HEINDEL**   Art Director: Bart Forbes   Client: Dallas Ballet Company   **SILVER MEDAL** and **HAMILTON KING AWARD**

SAN FRANCISCO OPERA
Kurt Herbert Adler, General Director

59 TH SEASON
1981

405   Artist: **MILTON GLASER**   Art Director: Milton Glaser   Client: The San Francisco Opera

406
Artist: **MICHAEL DAVID BROWN**
Client: Folger Library

The hair of frightened Icabod Crane rose up on his head **in terror**
"Who are you?" he demanded with s t a m m e r r i i nng voice.
There was no reply. "Who ARE You?" still no answer.
Though the night was **dark** and dismal he could just
make out what appeared to be a horseman of **Large** dimension
mounted on a **black** horse of **powerful** frame

But

against the sky
it could be seen that **the head**

Which should have rested on the shoulders was Carried before him
on the saddle!

His terror rose to Desperation...

407 Artist: **MICHAEL DAVID BROWN** Client: Virginia Lithograph

408 Artist: **HODGES SOILEAU** Art Director: Hodges Soileau Client: Artists Associates

409 Artist: **DON IVAN PUNCHATZ** Art Director: Steve Harding Client: Granada **SILVER MEDAL**

410
Artist: **STEVE SHOCK**
Client: Hellman Design

411 Artist: **HAROLD WIND**

412
Artist: **SIMMS TABACK**
Art Director: Ellen Rongstad
Magazine: Let's Find Out

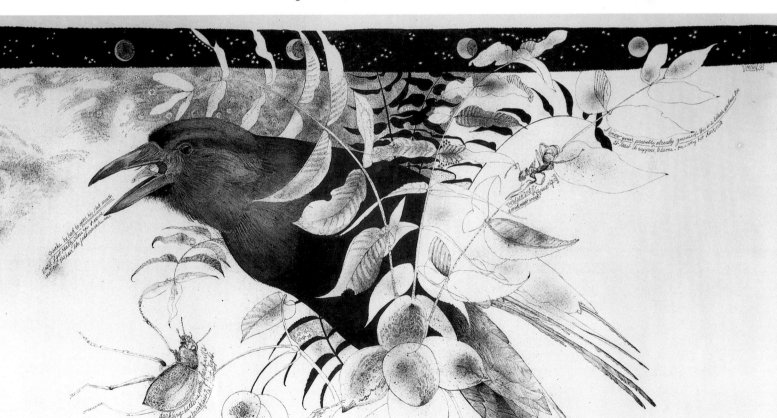

413   Artist: **JACK UNRUH**   Art Director: Dean Pingrey   Agency: Willis Case Harwood, Inc.   Client: Mead Paper

414
Artist: **HOWARD KOSLOW**
Art Director: W. Kirtman Plummer
Client: The Franklin Mint

415
Artist: **ROBERT JOHN BYRD**
Art Director: Jack Byrne
Client: Armstrong Cork

416
Artist: **FRED OTNES**
Art Director: W. Kirtman Plummer
Client: The Franklin Mint

417 Artist: **CHARLES McVICKER**

418 Artist: **GERALD McCONNELL** Client: Royal Saudi Air Force

419 Artist: **JACQUIE MARIE VAUX**

420 Artist: **JOE ISOM** Client: Breckenridge Resort Association

421
Artist: **MARK ENGLISH**
Client: The Miller Brewing Co.

422
Artist: **MARK ENGLISH**
Client: The Miller Brewing Co.

423
Artist: **PAUL GIOVANOPOULOS**
Art Director: J.A. Zisson
Agency: Arton Associates, Inc.
Client: J.A. Zisson

424   Artist: **LINDA CROCKETT-HANZEL**

425
Artist: **ROBERT HEINDEL**
Art Director: Mark English

426
Artist: **STEVE SHOCK**
Art Director: Gary Kelley
Client: Hellman Design

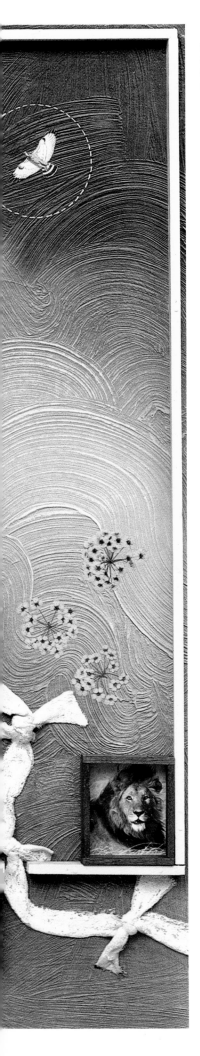

427
Artist: **TOM BOOKWALTER**
Art Director: Ralph Robinson
Client: CUNA Mutual Insurance Group

428
Artist: **VIDA PAVESICH**
Client: Vida Pavesich

429
Artist: **DEANNA GLAD**

430
Artist: **BARBARA NESSIM**
Art Director: Shinichiro Tora
Client: Hotel Barmen's Association, Japan

431
Artist: **RICHARD ELY**
Art Director: Richard Ely
Client: Zoma Gallery

432
Artist: **RICHARD ELY**
Art Director: Richard Ely
Client: Rizzoli International Bookstores

433
Artist: **GEORGE GIUSTI**
Art Director: Shinichiro Tora
Client: Hotel Barmen's Association, Japan

434
Artist: **DOUG JOHNSON**
Art Director: George Grudzicki
Client: Burlington Menswear

436 Artists: **JEMERSON/BETH YAKEY**   Art Director: David Young   Agency: Pearson Group   Client: Indiana Credit Union League

437 Artist: **DONNI GIAMBRONE**   Art Director: Don Dubowski   Client: Hallmark Cards, Inc.

438 Artist: **LINDA CROCKETT-HANZEL**

440   Artist: **CHRISTOPHER HERON**   Art Director: Christopher Heron
Client: Onondaga Public Library

441
Artist: **STAN WATTS**
Art Director: Roger Carpenter
Client: Papermoon Graphics

439
Artist: **DARRELL SWEET**
Art Director: Donald E. Munson
Client: Ballantine Books

442
Artist: **BILL NELSON**
Art Director: Bill Nelson
Client: Coleman for Governor

443
Artist: **RICHARD HERNÁNDEZ**
Art Director: Richard Hernández

444
Artist: **BILL VUKSANOVICH**
Art Director: Bill Vuksanovich

445
Artist: **KIRSTEN SODERLIND**
Client: Steve Collier

446
Artist: **GERALD J. MONLEY, JR.**
Art Directors: Al Evans/John Dudek
Client: World Color Press

447
Artist: **PETER McCAFFREY**
Art Director: Marshall Arisman
Client: Vision Art Students Work of USA

448
Artist: **ROBERT A. OLSON**
Art Director: Tina Adamek
Client: Lindenmeyr Paper

449
Artist: **EDWARD SOREL**
Art Director: Edward Sorel
Client: Bäckströms Repro

450
Artist: **LINDA CROCKETT-HANZEL**

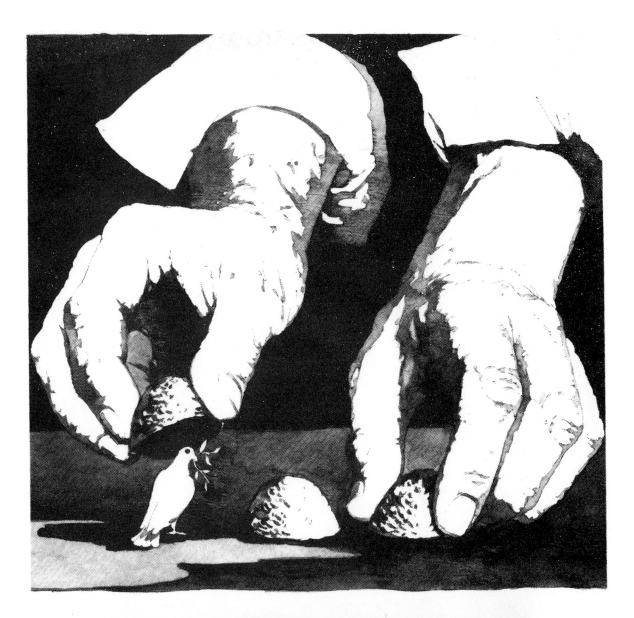

451 Artist: **SAUL LAMBERT** Client: Jane Lander Associates

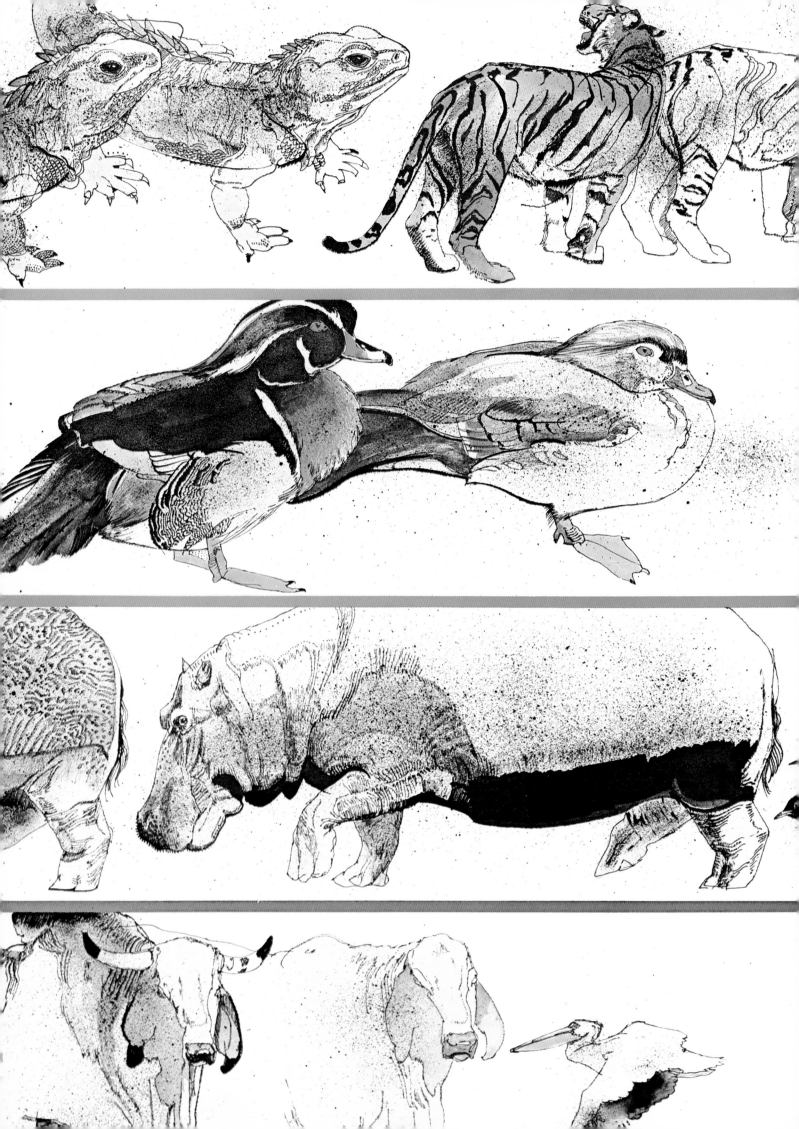

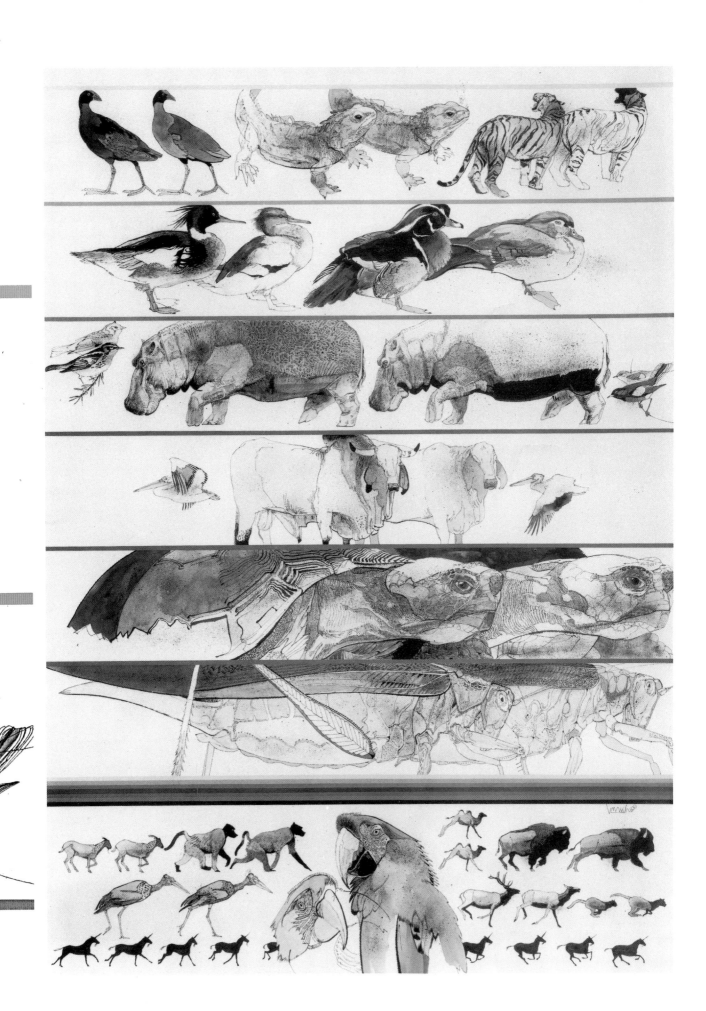

452 Artist: **JACK UNRUH** Art Director: André Sala Publisher: Portal Publications, Ltd.

453
Artist: **MURRAY TINKELMAN**
Client: ADDY Awards

454
Artist: **JOHN RUSH**
Art Director: John Rush
Client: Pema Browne Ltd.

455 Artist: **THOMAS A. GIESEKE** Art Director: Nicholas N. Brocker Client: The Great Western Drawing Co.

456 Artist: **THOMAS R. BLACKSHEAR, II** Art Director: Scott Service Client: Coors Beer

457 Artist: **THOMAS R. BLACKSHEAR, II** Client: Godbold/Richter Studios

458   Artist: **MARA McAFEE**

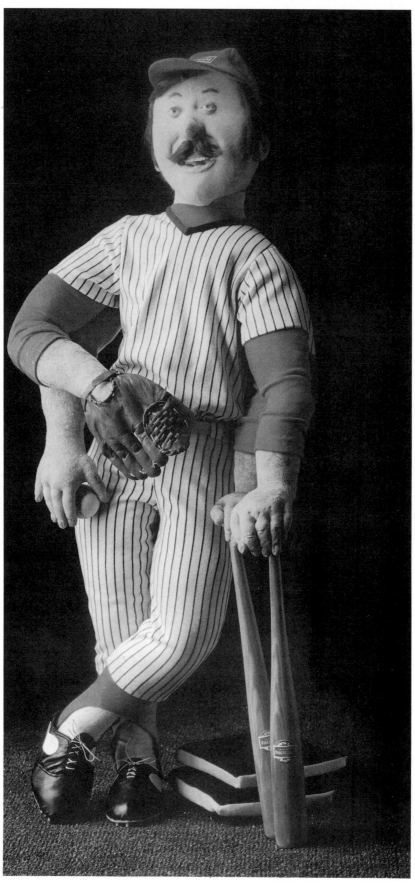

459 Artist: **ELLEN RIXFORD**
Art Director: Vyto Bendoraitis   Agency: Fahlgren & Ferris   Client: Owens Corning Glass

460 Artist: **WALT SPITZMILLER**
Art Director: Walt Spitzmiller   Client: Spectrum Fine Arts Gallery

461 Artist: **ROGER BURKHART** Client: Padgett Printing Corporation

462 Artist: **ANDREW GASKILL**

463
Artist: **FRANK J. CANNAS**
Art Director: John Urbain
Client: E. Butson P.M.I.

464   Artist: **BART FORBES**   Art Directors: Dennis Heath/David Sturgiss   Client: Mid-Continent Supply Company

465
Artist: **MURRAY TINKELMAN**
Art Director: Richard B. Luden
Agency: Sweet & Co.
Client: Murray Tinkelman

466 Artist: **PETER COX**

467 Artist: **LARRY WINBORG**   Client: Ralph Brinton

468 Artist: **LARRY WINBORG**   Client: George Pallotta

469 Artist: **BART FORBES**   Art Director: Dean Pingrey   Agency: Willis, Case, Harwood Advertising   Client: Mead Paper Company

470
Artist: **JOHN MURPHY**
Art Director: Deborah Anderson
Client: Connecticut Public Television

471
Artist: **PAUL MELIA**
Art Director: Jim Conley
Client: Armco, Inc.

472 Artist: **JOHN M. THOMPSON**   Art Director: Scott Service   Client: Coors Beer

473
Artist: **MIMI VANG OLSEN**
Art Director: Mimi Vang Olsen
Client: Carolyn Bean Publishing

474
Artist: **GARY KELLEY**
Art Director: Gary Kelley
Client: Hellman Designs

475
Artist: **LARRY WINBORG**
Client: David & Kathy Adams

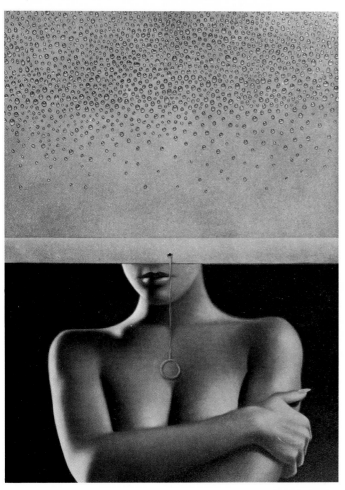

476 Artist: **DENNIS LUZAK**

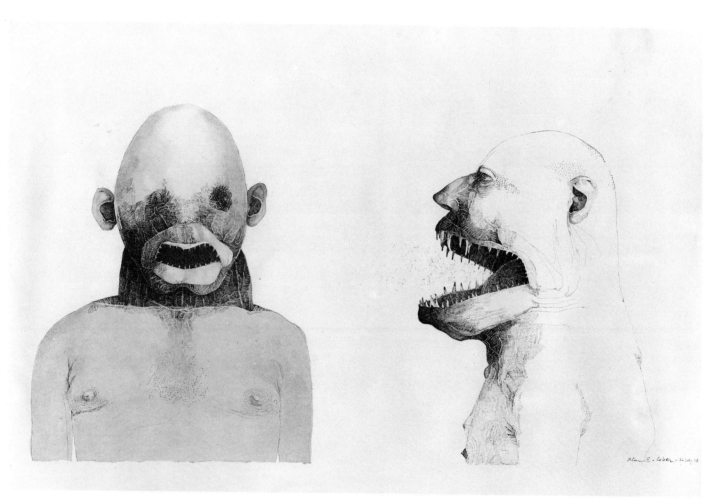

477 Artist: **ALAN E. COBER**   Art Director: Arbram Lenscob   Client: Bäckströms Repro

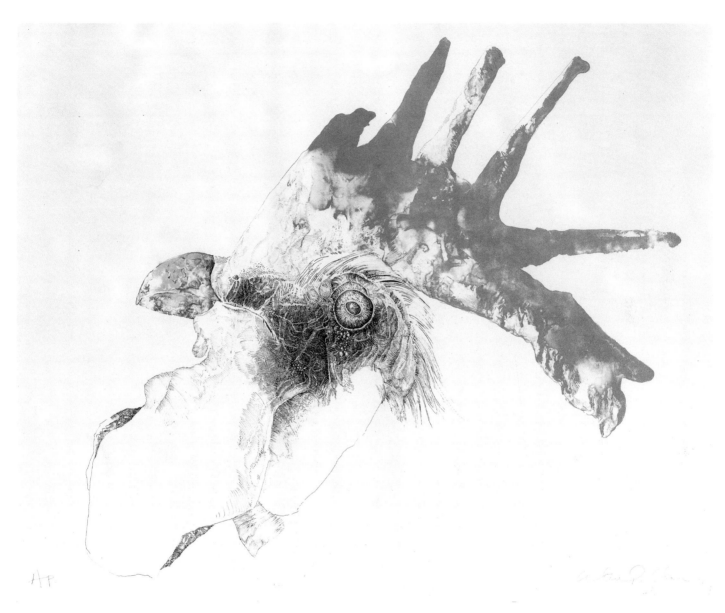

478 Artist: **ALAN E. COBER**

479 Artist: **LONNI SUE JOHNSON** Art Director: Alice Degenhardt Magazine: Creative Living

480 Artist: **MICHAEL DAVID BROWN** Client: Virginia Lithograph

481
Artist: **DARRELL SWEET**
Art Director: Donald E. Munson
Client: Ballantine Books

482 Artist: **JIM SHARPE**　Art Director: Michael Brent　Magazine: Tennis

483
Artists: **GRIESBACH/MARTUCCI**
Art Director: Debra Dailey
Publisher: St. Martin's Press

484
Artist: **BARBARA CARR**
Art Director: John deCesare
Client: The Illustrators Workshop

485 Artist: **KIRSTEN SODERLIND** Client: Patricia Stephenson

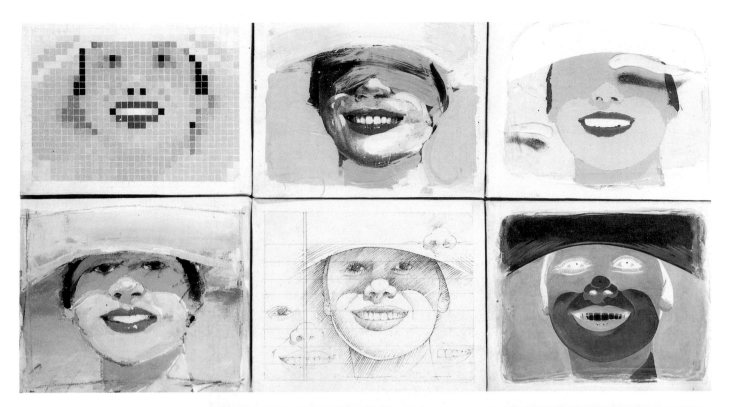

486
Artist: **PAUL GIOVANOPOULOS**
Art Director: J.A. Zisson
Agency: Arton Associates, Inc.
Client: J.A. Zisson

487   Artist: **KIRSTEN SODERLIND**   Client: Harvey Kahn & Assoc.

489 Artist: **BILL VUKSANOVICH**

490   Artist: **FRED OTNES**   Art Director: Nelson Pollack   Client: Gilbert Color Systems

491 Artist: **FRED OTNES** Art Director: Karen Katinas Client: Marsh & McLennan

492
Artists: **LEE & MARY SIEVERS**
Client: Wildlife Gallery

493   Artist: **JOHN M. KILROY**   Client: Carmark Fisheries

495 Artist: **JOHN BUXTON**

494
Artist: **JACK UNRUH**
Art Director: Carl Lively
Client: Supron

496 Artist: **ROBERT M. CUNNINGHAM** Art Director: Shinichiro Tora Client: Hotel Barmen's Association, Japan

Clara Barton, 1821-1912 … Humanitarian, founder of the American National Red Cross, and advocate of women's rights. Visit her home at Clara Barton National Historic Site in Glen Echo, Maryland. The area is administered by the National Park Service, United States Department of the Interior.

497 Artist: **MARK ENGLISH**   Art Director: Dennis McLaughlin   Client: National Park Service

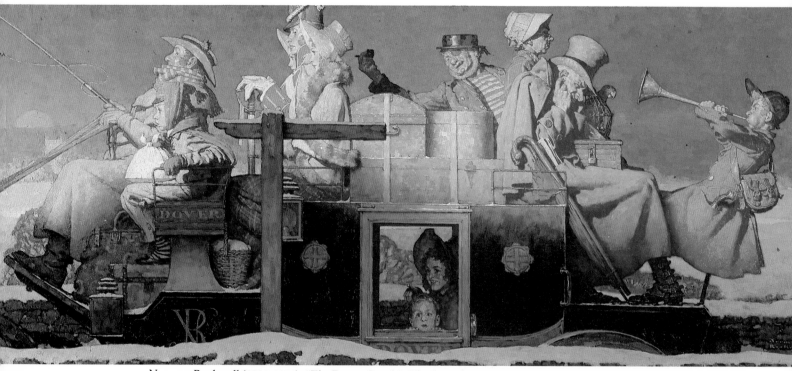

Norman Rockwell (1894-1978). "The Dover Coach", The Saturday Evening Post, 1935 donated by the artist

SOCIETY OF ILLUSTRATORS ACTIVITIES
THE MUSEUM OF AMERICAN ILLUSTRATION

The Permanent Collection of the Society's Museum of American Illustration continues to grow in quality and importance. It now contains 978 illustrations by 346 artists. It is the most comprehensive collection of any museum dedicated solely to the art of illustration.

This growth has been the product of the generous support of the membership and friends of the Society. Last year alone, the Museum was the recipient of 158 pieces including works by F.R. Gruger, James Montgomery Flagg, Coby Whitmore, Frank Vincent Dumond, Bob Peak, Mark English and Fred Otnes. The Society's purchases from a J. Walter Thompson Co. grant included a Howard Chandler Christy, a Dean Cornwell, a Walter Biggs and a Herbert Morton Stoops, among others. On permanent loan from the Yale University Art Gallery are five drawings by Edwin Austin Abbey.

This year the Museum Committee plans an aggressive acquisition program to expand its contemporary art collection.

The entire collection has been catalogued by Terrence Brown, SI Curator. Several important exhibitions have been assembled from the Permanent Collection by John Moodie, Chairman. Artwork has been loaned to the Brooklyn Museum, The Delaware Museum, Grand Central Galleries and General Electric Corporation under a policy of making available the best of illustration to a public that is becoming increasingly aware that it is not only an art form but a nostalgic, historical record of our past.

Future plans include a book cataloguing the complete collection with reproductions of the examples in color and an informative text describing the history of and tracing the changes in illustration for the past 100 years.

On these and the succeeding four pages are examples of illustration from the collection.

Museum Committee: Art Weithas, *Director;* John Moodie, *Chairman, Permanent Collection;*
(1981-1982)   Walt Reed, Howard Munce, Murray Tinkelman, Scott Reynolds

l. to r. John Witt, SI President, Arpi Ermoyan, Executive Director, Terrence Brown, Museum Curator, Art Weithas, Museum Director/Executive Vice President; John Moodie, Chairman of the Permanent Collection Committee.

photograph by John Manno

Joseph Christian Leyendecker (1874-1951)
"Easter", The Saturday Evening Post, 1934
donated by the artist

Newell Convers Wyeth (1882-1945)
"The Black Arrow", by Robert Louis Stevenson
Charles Scribner's Sons, 1910 donated by the artist

Dean Cornwell (1892-1960)
"Romance At One", Cosmopolitan Magazine, 1938
J. Walter Thompson Company Purchase Fund

Howard Chandler Christy (1873-1952)
"Fight Or Buy Bonds", Third Liberty Loan Poster, 1917
Society of Illustrators Members Purchase Fund

Charles Dana Gibson (1867-1944) "At The Recital" donated by C. D. Williams

Edwin Austin Abbey (1852-1960)
"The Heath", King Lear by William Shakespeare
Harper & Brothers, 1902
on loan from The Yale University Art Gallery

Russell Patterson (1896-1977) "Ladies Undressing"
donated by Mr. and Mrs. Abril Lamarque

Arthur William Brown (1881-1966)
"Mr. Tutt", The Saturday Evening Post, 1926
donated by the artist

James Montgomery Flagg (1877-1960)
"Mr. Simpson Directs" donated by the artist

Wallace Morgan (1873-1948)
"The Story of Cedric", Liberty Magazine
donated by the artist

Frederic R. Gruger (1871-1953)
"The Thunderer" by E. Garrington Harper's
Bazaar, 1926 donated by F. R. Gruger, Jr.

Harvey Dunn (1884-1952)
"Storming The Bastille" donated by the artist

Stevan Dohanos, B. 1907 "The Coal Men",
The Saturday Evening Post, donated by the artist

Mead Schaeffer (1898-1980) "The Highway Men",
The American Magazine, 1957 donated by the artist

Al Parker, B. 1906 "Black and White Swimsuit"
donated by the artist

Coby Whitmore, B. 1913
"Love is a Bargain", Ladies Home Journal, 1947
J. Walter Thompson Company Purchase Fund

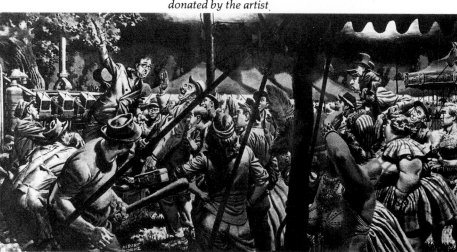

Al Dorne (1904-1965) "Mr. Botts, Tractor Salesman",
The Saturday Evening Post,
donated by Edna Dorne

Mark English b. 1933
"Nude's Back" donated by the artist

Robert M. Cunningham b. 1924
"Pilgrim at Tinker Creek"
Sports Illustrated, 1974
donated by the artist

Bernie Fuchs b. 1932
"The Walking Circus"
The Franklin Library, 1978
anonymous donation

Fred Otnes b. 1926
"Play Ball", Sports Illustrated,
1977 donated by the artist

Harold von Schmidt (1893-1982)
"The Horse Race",
Esquire Magazine, 1950
donated by the artist

Bob Peak b. 1928
"Jackie Stewart", Sports Illustrated,
1974 donated by the artist

ANNUAL STUDENT SCHOLARSHIP COMPETITION

The Society of Illustrators Annual Scholarship Competition
1982

Matt Mahurin
Art Center College of Design
Elizabeth Sweeney, Instructor
$1500 Society of Illustrators Award
Top Left

Jon Post
Kendall School of Design
Robert Divita, Instructor
$1500 The Starr Foundation Award
Top Right

Kathy Schermer
California State University, Fullerton
Larry Johnson, Instructor
$1500 Lila Acheson Wallace Award
Bottom Right

The Annual Student Scholarship Competition and Exhibition sponsored by the Society of Illustrators has, over the past 20 years, evolved into one of our most rewarding projects. From its modest beginnings, it has blossomed into a competition which involves artwork submitted from over 110 colleges, universities and art schools representing almost all of the fifty states in this country.

The artwork, submitted in 35mm slide form, encompasses the entire gamut of illustration. Paintings, drawings, collages, use of new mechanical techniques and influences, reflect the wide interest of today's art student.

Over 4,300 entries were submitted in the 1982 competition. The jury, consisting of twelve professional illustrators, spent many hours viewing these slides in order to select the outstanding pieces of art to be exhibited and those to receive awards. Twenty thousand dollars were distributed among 42 students. This sum was reached by combining the proceeds from a Christmas auction of artwork contributed by Society members, and two grants; one from Lila Acheson Wallace of the Reader's Digest, the other from The Starr Foundation. Society members also contributed individual amounts for awards in their names. The Hallmark Foundation underwrote the expense of the exhibition and contributed matching grants to the schools of the award winning students.

For the second year a brochure, also underwritten by Hallmark, showing all the artwork in the exhibition, was prepared by the Society, and was ready for distribution at the Awards Presentation ceremony. This catalog will take its place in a continuing record of this annual event.

The Society of Illustrators is both proud and honored to offer illustrators of the future a showplace for their efforts, and to bring them to the attention of the illustrator's world.

Alvin J. Pimlser
Chairman, Education Committee

Left to Right: John Witt, President of Society of Illustrators; George Parker and Arch Unruh, of Hallmark; Robert H. Blattner, of Readers Digest and Alvin Pimsler, Chairman Scholarship Committee

John Roberts of The Starr Foundation

EXHIBITIONS

It was a banner year for exhibitions in the SI Museum's new gallery. Aside from the Society's Annual National Exhibition and the Student Scholarship Exhibition, there were a select number of shows that reflected the best of contemporary and classic illustration.

Among the "one-man" exhibitors were Alan E. Cober, Bob Ziering, Fred Otnes and Ned Seidler.

The "group" shows included "The Pictorial History of the U.S. Air Force" and the "Artist in the Parks", both exhibits by Society members. "The Chicago School", a nostalgic show of the '20's and '30's, included works by Haddon Sundblom, Harry Anderson, Andrew Loomis, Ed Henry, Coby Whitmore and many others — an historically important page in the history of American Illustration.

The final exhibition was of the Society's new acquisitions. There were 145 pieces in the show, including two Edwin Austin Abbeys on permanent loan from Yale University Art Gallery. The Society of Illustrators wishes to express its gratitude to the members and patrons whose generous donations to the Heritage Collection made this exhibition possible. Bernie Karlin designed the catalog for this exhibition.

Scott Reynolds, as Chairman of the Exhibition Committee, did a superb job of hanging the various exhibits.

Gallery 3, a showcase for SI members, had some outstanding exhibitions scheduled by Chairman Mike Hooks: Murray Tinkelman, Carl Lundgren, Keith Reynolds, Ed Renfro, Mike Quon, Sandy Huffaker, Scott Reynolds, Naiad Einsel, Charles McVicker, Chris Spollen, Roland Descombes, Dennis Luzak, Wayne Barlowe and Craig Tennant.

Photos: Bill Frazer

Opening reception for exhibition "3D and Magic Realism" at the Society of Illustrators Museum of American Illustration.

New Acquisitions Exhibition. l. to r. Mrs. Jack Ruge, Contributors, Carol Wald, Naiad Einsel and Walter Einsel.

Opening reception for the "Pictorial History of the U.S. Air Force". l. to r. John Witt, SI President; Alice Price, Chief, Art and Museum Branch USAF; Keith Ferris, Chairman Government Services Committee; Brigadier General Richard F. Abel, USAF Director of Public Affairs; Don Moss, Co-Chairman, Air Force Committee.

Hanging the 24th Annual Exhibition. Scott Reynolds, Exhibition Chairman, Richard Sparks and Amy Huelsman assisting.

Photo: Terrence Brown

New Acquisitions Exhibition. Contributor, Everett Raymond Kinstler.

John Dockery, announcer for WNET-TV, in the Society's Museum Gallery during taping of special "Big Apple" TV spot.

Photo: Terrence Brown

Opening reception for Fred Otnes exhibition. l. Fred Otnes, r. Robert Heindel.

SI LIBRARY OF AMERICAN ILLUSTRATION

With the Museum now successfully operational, the Society has undertaken fundraising for construction of this important new entity.

The facility will occupy the Founders Room on the fourth floor and will incorporate the existing Norman Price Library.

Upon completion, it will contain shelving for thousands of books, storage areas for archival material, a slide and film section and a system for information and pictorial reference retrieval.

The new library will be open to members and qualified researchers by appointment.

PUBLISHING

Looking ahead into the eighties, the Society of Illustrators plans to become even more active in its publishing efforts. Encouraged by the response to its special project books such as "200 Years of American Illustration" and "20 Years of Award Winners", several new ventures are being considered for the coming years. The emphasis will be, of course, on informing the illustration community about the history of this art form and the contributions made by its practitioners.

The Museum wing of the Society is compiling one of the finest collections of American illustration in the country. These works will undoubtedly be published some time in the near future. The Society also plans to continue its "Library of American Illustration" series, whose first two volumes, "Magic and Other Realism" and "Illustration in the Third Dimension" were so well received.

This Annual Book, "Illustrators 24", is the second volume produced solely by the Society and its members. As an organization experiencing a period of tremendous growth, the Society feels it should enter into the arena of self-publication, adding yet another dimension to its usefulness to the art community at large.

Gerald McConnell
Publishing Director

SI ANNUAL ART AUCTION

Hundreds of original works of art, representing a wide range of historic and contemporary illustration, are available at affordable prices.

This public event held in the Museum galleries in mid-December is also a major source of funding for our Student Scholarship Awards.

PUBLICITY

The Museum was featured in one of a series of TV spots called, "The Big Apple" (Channel 5), showing some of the delightful activities of New York City.

Keith Ferris, Chairman of the Society's Government Services Committee, appeared on a half hour presentation for WOR-TV.

Artist's rendering by Barnett Plotkin of the Society's Proposed New Library of American Illustration.

POLICE ATHLETIC LEAGUE ART COMPETITION

Walter Hortens, long a judge for this annual event, has incorporated this activity for high school artists into our educational and community service programs.

This year, Jerry McDaniel, another concerned SI member and juror, was able to provide a full scholarship for one of the student winners to the Columbus College of Art & Design in Ohio.

In addition, the Society has donated cash awards to supplement those of the Police Athletic League.

SI EVENING WORKSHOPS

These informal sessions, held 3 nights a week in our top floor studio, provide an opportunity for artists of all experience to work side by side on portrait, figure and fashion models.

An exhibition of these works was displayed in the members' gallery in July.

Photos: Constance Witt

Monday night portrait classes.

Thursday night fashion classes.

HAROLD von SCHMIDT (1893-1982)
President of the Society of Illustrators 1938-1941
Honorary President 1966-1982
Portrait by James Montgomery Flagg

As I pondered where to possibly begin on the subject of this giant, a persistent visual image loomed over me; it was the word VON spelled out in monumental piled stones reaching to the sky — the kind of thing movies often do in their ads for larger-than-life epics.

Von's role in the history of illustration qualifies him for that kind of lofty and rarified image.

I shall pass over the myriad civic, athletic, teaching and military endeavors covered in his obituaries — then leave to you to read elsewhere in two excellent books, his rugged exploits and adventures in the long-ago West.

I'll try to do him justice by simply stating a bit of what I observed in the 47 years I knew him — from the day I first called upon him as a high school kid with a meager collection of amateur efforts.

Two things stand out from that long-ago day; he didn't talk down — his remarks contained quotes from unknowns to me — like Pyle and Dunn.

And he said of my attempts, "These are only fragments — you must learn to make *pictures*".

That sentence echoes still.

It might surprise those of you who never heard him talk, that this ex-cowpuncher who dealt regularly with action, violence and adventure in his work, used the beautiful work *design* repeatedly. It was inherent in him.

Von started with that sensibility bred in his bones and later added to it his extraordinary draftsmanship, his vast knowledge of the West and the Indian, his historical thirst for accuracy and authenticity, his remarkable depiction of country and place, his sharp observer's eye and his natural bent as a story teller. Those qualities produced the man who produced a lifetime of pictures that remain among the best of their genre.

How ironic that this gifted man should see in his latter ill and inactive years the astronomical rise in value and favor of a flood of lesser western art hyped by gushers of money from fat cats in the new West and in Hollywood.

But there's a happy side — for few other artists have ever been so thoroughly praised, honored and revered as Von was in his lifetime.

His friends, his profession, his town celebrated his achievements and offered him homage over and over again. Obituaries don't catch that kind of thing.

One lovely spring day when I visited him a couple of years back, we sat at his picture window facing a stream and a small patch of woods. I remarked that it must have been a revelation when he first arrived in verdant New England from the arid West to discover the lushness of this place. His answer was, "The first day we moved in I walked into that patch and in just a couple yards I counted *eighteen different greens!*"

May the count rise even higher.

Howard Munce

INDEX

ARTISTS

Palan, Michael R., 40
7330 Montour St.
Philadelphia, PA 19111

Palencar, John Jude, 49
6763 Middlebrook Blvd.
Middleburg, Hts., OH 44130

Palulian, Dickran, 283, 384
18 McKinley St.
Rowayton, CT 06853

Pardue, Jack, 81, 313, 389
2307 Sherwood Hall Lane
Alexandria, VA 22306

Parker, Robert Andrew, 39, 120
Jennings Rd.
South Kent, CT 06785

Pate, Martin, 11
1700 Golden Gate Dr. NW
Atlanta, GA 30309

Pavesich, Vida, 428
81 Hamilton Place
Oakland, CA 94612

Payne, Christopher F., 93
306 Nettle Dr.
Garland, TX 75043

Peak, Bob, 254, 255,256, 270
c/o Harvey Kahn
50 East 50 St.
NYC, NY 10022

Pedersen, Judy, 123
96 Greene St.
NYC, NY 10012

Pels, Winslow Pinney, 330, 370
226 East 53 St.
NYC, NY 10022

Pertchik, Harriet, 96
21 Sinclair Martin Dr.
Rosyln, NY 11576

Pfeiffer, Fred, 177
444 South Kingsley Dr.
Los Angeles, CA 90020

Pienkos, Jeff, 367
503 Smith Ave.
Lake Bluff, IL 60044

Pinkney, Jerry, 33, 139, 331, 371, 395
41 Furnace Dock Rd.
Croton-on-Hudson, NY 10520

Pisano, Al, 318
21 Skyline Dr.
Upper Saddle River, NJ 07458

Plotkin, Barnett, 298
126 Wooleys Lane
Great Neck, NY 11023

Powell, Ivan, 280
58 West 15 St.
NYC, NY 10011

Punchatz, Don Ivan, 169, 337, 347, 409
2605 Westgage
Arlington, TX 76015

Radigan, Bob, 339
742 Pyrula Ave.
Sanibel Island, FL 33957

Reid, Charles, 107
Box 113
Greens Farms, CT 06436

Reingold, Alan, 312
331 West 71 St.
NYC, NY 10023

Reynolds, William G., 386
5629 Abbott Ave. S
Edina, MN 55410

Ribes, Fredericka, 121
203 Seventh Ave.
Brooklyn, NY 11215

Rixford, Ellen, 334, 459
308 West 97 St.
NYC, NY 10025

Roberts, Stanley, 10
16 Irene St.
Burlington, MA 01803

Rodanas, Kristina, 202, 204
28 Ridge Rd.
West Barnstable, MA 02668

Rosetti, Mario A., 276
230 Stark Rd.
Cloquet, MN 55720

Rush, John, 60, 454
123 Kedzie St.
Evanston, IL 60202

Sabin, Tracy, 376
281 Countrywood Lane
Encinitas, CA 92024

Santore, Charles, 281, 297
138 South 20 St.
Philadelphia, PA 19103

Saso, Frank, 358
3163 San Mateo St.
Clearwater, FL 33519

Sauter, Ron, 274, 390
328 Brett Rd.
Rochester, NY 14609

Schoenherr, John, 86
RD #2 Box 260
Stockton, NJ 08559

Schwartz, Daniel, 3, 251
48 East 13 St.
NYC, NY 10003

Scribner, Joanne L., 197, 203
N. 3314 Lee
Spokane, WA 99207

Seaver, Jeff, 311
130 West 24 St.
NYC, NY 10011

Seidler, Ned, 111
c/o National Geographic Society
1145 17 St. NW
Washington, D.C. 20036

Seltzer, Isadore, 64
336 Central Park West
NYC, NY 10025

Sharpe, Jim, 25, 482
5 Side Hill Rd.
Westport, CT 06880

Shay, R.J., 79
343 Hillside Ave.
St. Louis, MO 63119

Shikler, Aaron, 4
c/o David & Long
746 Madison Ave.
NYC, NY 10021

Shilstone, Arthur, 326
42 Picketts Ridge Rd.
West Redding, CT 06896

Shock, Steve, 410, 426
Hellman Design Associates
1225 West 4 St.
Waterloo, IA 50702

Siegel, Ellyn, 124
39 Concord Rd.
Danbury, CT 06810

Sievers, Lee, 492
5516 Queen Ave. SO
Minneapolis, MN 55410

Sievers, Mary, 492
5516 Queen Ave. SO
Minneapolis, MN 55410

Silverman, Burt, 80, 253, 299
324 West 71 St.
NYC, NY 10023

Skardinski, Stan, 125
251 West 30 St.
NYC, NY 10001

Smith, Brett, 327
c/o Frank & Jeff Lavaty
45 East 51 St.
NYC, NY 10022

Soderlind, Kirsten, 372, 445, 485, 487
1568 Second Ave.
NYC, NY 10028

Soileau, Hodges, 408
350 Flax Hill Rd.
Norwalk, CT 06854

Sorel, Edward, 73, 172, 173, 174, 449
137 East 56 St.
NYC, NY 10022

Soyer, Raphael, 126
54 West 74 St.
NYC, NY 10023

Spanfeller, Jim, 47, 220, 287
Mustato, Rd.
Katonah, NY 10536

Sparks, Richard, 69, 94, 103, 238, 277
Two West Rocks Road
Norwalk, CT 06851

Spitzmiller, Walt, 349, 360, 460
24 Lee Lane
West Redding, CT 06896

Spollen, Chris, 51
203 Center St.
Staten Island, NY 10306

Steele, Robert G., 138, 181, 183
1537 Franklin St.
San Francisco, CA 94109

Stemelo, Kathleen, 20, 77
188 East 93 St.
NYC, NY 10028

Stephens, Bill, 274, 390
328 Brett Rd.
Rochester, NY 14609

Stinson, Paul, 284
7 Stanford Dr.
Bridgewater, NJ 08807

Storey, Barron, 108
250 Mercer St.
NYC, NY 10012

Sumichrast, Susan, 289
860 North Northwoods Dr.
Deerfield, IL 60015

Sweet, Darrell, 114, 168, 439, 481
Pine Brae Dr.
Montgomery Township
Skillman, NJ 08558

Taback, Simms, 412
38 East 21 St.
NYC, NY 10010

Taggart, Beatrice, 346
c/o Carlson
67 Thompson St.
NYC, NY 10012

Tauss, Herbert, 175, 187, 234
South Mountain Pass
Garrison, NY 10524

Thompson, John M., 149, 150, 165,
River Road   292, 472
West Cornwall, CT 06796

Tinkelman, Murray, 145, 146, 147,
75 Lakeview Ave. W   453, 465
Peekskill, NY 10566

Tucker, Ezra N., 188
8427 Drury Circle
Kansas City, MO 64132

Unruh, Jack, 345, 413, 452, 494
2706 Fairmount
Dallas, TX 75201

Vaux, Jacquie Marie, 419
783 Santa Rose Plaza
Santa Rose, CA 95401

Vincent, Eric, 206
2902 Renshaw
Houston, TX 77023

Viskupic, Gary, 45, 230
7 Westfield Dr.
Centerport, NY 11727

Vuksanovich, Bill, 444, 489
3224 North Nordica
Chicago, IL 60634

Wack, Jeff, 294, 328
11950 Laurelwood Dr.
Studio City, CA 91604

Wald, Carol, 227, 271, 272, 381
57 East 78 St.
NYC, NY 10021

Waldman, Bruce, 235
751 President St.
Brooklyn, NY 11215

Waldman, Neil, 178
12 Turner Rd.
Pearl River, NY 10965

Walker, Norman, 61, 261
37 Stonehenge Rd.
Weston, CT 06883

Watts, Stan, 441
3896 San Marcos
Newberry Park, CA 91320

Welkis, Allen, 316
53 Heights Rd.
Fort Salonga, NY 11768

Weller, Don, 354
2427 Park Oak Dr.
Los Angeles, CA 90068

Wells, Charles, 312
P.O. Box 222
Washington Crossing, PA 18977

Welt, Susan, 189, 190
208 East 88 St.
NYC, NY 10028

Werneke, Angela, 200
Route 1, Box 81C
Santa Fe, NM 87501

Whalley, John, 184
P.O. Box 71
Harrison Valley, PA 16927

Whelan, Michael, 207, 218
172 Candlewood Lake Road
Brookfield, CT 06804

Whitcombe, Mark, 105
577 Minneford Ave.
City Island, NY 10464

White, Jim, 92, 231
6232 Forest Ave.
Hammond, IN 46324

Wilcox, David, 88, 387
P.O. Box 232
Califon, NJ 07830

Wilkin, Eloise, 201
504 Suburban Ct.
Rochester, NY 14620

ART DIRECTORS

CLIENTS

AGENCIES

MAGAZINES, PUBLISHERS, PUBLICATIONS

May I tell you a little bit about Time-Life Books' attitude toward commissioned art...

We don't just illustrate stories
and decorate pages.
We use art to communicate information.
We use art when a photograph won't do,
or just plain isn't available.
Art in a Time-Life Book is there to serve the reader.
Its function is to help the reader understand
some special aspect of our story.
It's a tool to enlighten and inform.
We're always looking for illustrators
who have strong interests in specialized fields,
such as medical, mechanical, historical,
geological, botanical or biological subjects.
Artists with special interests
bring a certain expertise to their work.
It reflects in the final product.
This is what we believe has made Time-Life Books
so outstanding.
If our concepts appeal to you,
we'd like to see your portfolio . . . call

TIME-LIFE BOOKS INC.
777 Duke Street
Alexandria, Virginia 22314
(703) 960-5200

Alan E. Cohen

By Fuchs,

NICHOLAS GAETANO

Gerstein

WILSON McLEAN:

B. Peak

Isadore Seltzer

Harvey Kahn Associates, Inc.

50 E.50 st. New York, New York 10022 212-752-8490
Doug Kahn, Associate

What do all these brushes have in common?

The Strathmore Kolinsky (#585)
The finest Kolinsky hair. Extraordinary natural spring and point.

WATERCOLOR

The Strathmore Red Sable (#485) Wash (#450)
The next best to our Kolinsky. Excellent spring and holds a good amount of color.

WATERCOLOR

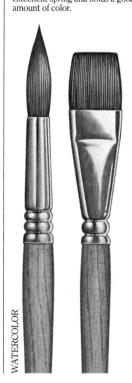

The Strathmore Sabeline (#385) Wash (#386)
The finest European Sabeline hair. Good spring and natural point. Inexpensive.

WATERCOLOR

The Strathmore Squirrel (#115)
Untrimmed French-dressed natural hair forms a needle-point tip. Inexpensive.

WATERCOLOR

The Strathmore White (#245) Wash (#230)
The highest quality synthetic fiber. Clean, sharp working edges.

WATERCOLOR

The Strathmore Sabeline (#390 & #395)
The finest European Sabeline hair. Excellent performance with good spring and sharp point.

OIL & ACRYLIC

The Strathmore Red Sable (#490 & #495)
Excellent natural spring and sharp point. Ideal for fine work of oil painting.

OIL & ACRYLIC

The Strathmore White (#250 & #285)
Top quality synthetic fiber. Good spring and sharp working edge.

OIL & ACRYLIC

The Strathmore Fine Quality Hog Bristle (#620, #610 & #615)
Designed with interlocking formation with natural Hog Bristle. High quality silky hair, springs back to original shape.

OIL & ACRYLIC

The Strathmore Superior Quality Hog Bristle (#640, #630 & #625)
The highest quality Chung King Bristle. Designed with the natural curve of the hair to interlock, giving extra spring. Each hair has unique natural split to hold more color. The ultimate quality for oil painting.

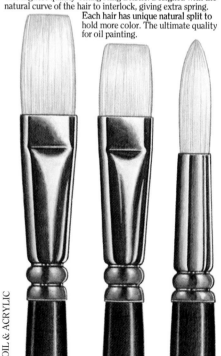

Strathmore Quality.

A Strathmore brush outperforms every other brush in its class.

FRED OTNES

Winner of over 50 awards from the
Society of Illustrators, New York

Represented by Bill Erlacher, Artists Associates
211 East 51st Street, New York, NY 10019
212-755-1365

illustration *noyes*

BILL ERLACHER ARTISTS ASSOCIATES

211 EAST 51 STREET, NEW YORK, NEW YORK 10022 (212) 755-1365/6 ASSOCIATE: NICOLE EDELL

ARTISTS REPRESENTED

NORMAN ADAMS

DON BRAUTIGAM

MICHAEL DEAS

MARK ENGLISH

ALEX GNIDZIEJKO

ROBERT HEINDEL

STEVE KARCHIN

DICK KREPEL

SKIP LIEPKE

RICK McCOLLUM

FRED OTNES

DANIEL SCHWARTZ

Carol Wald

The Society of Illustrators
expresses its appreciation to
Dai Nippon for its fine spirit of
cooperation and the excellent
quality of reproduction in this, our
24th Annual of American Illustration,
as well as for Illustrators 23, the
Society's first venture
in producing its own book.

*This year's beautifully conceived book sets the highest standard
of excellence in choice and reproduction; a yardstick by which we
all measure our talents and our best achievements. I am always proud
to be included in the Society of Illustrators' Annuals.*

CAROL WALD

*Dai Nippon is regarded most highly by the graphic professionals
in Japan because of their high quality products and services.
This was well demonstrated in the quality and services they
promised in producing the Society's 23rd Annual.
I certainly had a great deal of experience in working with the Dai
Nippon when I was working in Japan, and am pleased that they are
extending their capabilities in the U.S.*

*KO NODA
KoNoda & Associates; International*

*It is a pleasure to see superior work by gifted artists reproduced
so faithfully. The talent represented in this year's Society of
Illustrators Annual deserves the superior conception and execution that
it is given. My artists and I thank you.*

*Harvey Kahn
Harvey Kahn Associates, Artists Representatives*

*To work with Dai Nippon is to work in harmony and toward the same goal:
excellence. I am completely impressed with their professionalism and
their attention to every detail. These people really care.*

Gerald McConnell

**DNP (America), Inc.
1633 Broadway, 15th Fl.
New York, N.Y. 10019**

**Dai Nippon Printing Co., Ltd.
1-12, Ichigaya Kagacho, Shinjuku-ku
Tokyo, 162 Japan**
International Sales Division 1-12 Ichigaya Kagacho, Shinjuku-ku
Tokyo, Japan

New York - Chicago - Santa Clara - San Francisco - Sydney - Hong
Kong - Jakarta - Singapore - Düsseldorf - London

....ABOARD THE S.S. FAIRWIND IN THE CARIBBEAN FOR SITMAR CRUISES

THIS IS HOW BOB HEINDEL LOOKS WHEN HE WORKS

TO LOOK AT BOB HEINDEL'S WORK...SEE NOS. 28, 44, 308, 366, 404, 425

TO SEE MORE...CONTACT: BILL ERLACHER
ARTISTS ASSOCIATES
211 EAST 51 STREET
NEW YORK, NY 10022
212 755-1365/6

ARE YOU A POTENTIAL SUPERSTAR ?

Isn't it about time you found out? Syracuse University's Independent Study Degree Program gives you an opportunity to work toward your MFA in Advertising Design or Illustration while you're working full time. And you study face-to-face with the top designers and illustrators in the industry.

For two weeks each summer (for three summers) you study with superstars like the former faculty listed below. The rest of the year you're working on independent study assignments and making a few long-weekend field trips to study with the top communicators right where they live and work. Places like New York, Toronto, Chicago and London.

You'll find out more about how the pros work, you'll make more connections and you'll learn more than you can possibly imagine.

For information contact: Director, Syracuse University ISDP / **Room 45.** 610 E. Fayette Street / Syracuse, N.Y. 13202 / (315) 423-3269.

Study with the pros ALLAN BEAVER, JOE BOWLER, TOM CARNASE, MILTON CHARLES, STEVE COSMOPULOS, PAUL DAVIS, LOU DORFSMAN, GENE FEDERICO, DICK GANGEL, AMIL GARGANO, BOB GROSSMAN, DICK HARVEY, BOB HEINDEL, DOUG JOHNSON, DICK HESS, HELMUT KRONE, HERB LUBALIN, WILSON McCLEAN, JIM McMULLAN, JACQUI MORGAN, DAVE PASSALACQUA, ARTHUR PAUL, LARRY PLAPLER, SHIRLEY POLYKOFF, HEIDI RICKABAUGH, SAM SCALI, EILEEN HEDY SCHULTZ, ISADORE SELTZER, BERT STEINHAUSER, MURRAY TINKELMAN, DON TROUSDELL & ROBERT WEAVER

DANIEL SCHWARTZ

Represented by: Bill Erlacher, Artists Associates   211 East 51 Street New York, N.Y. 10022
(212) 755-1365/6

Edwin Austin Abbey

Henry Raleigh

ILLUSTRATION from A to Z

We make a market in illustration art, by both buying and selling the originals of American illustrators. Covering the whole history of the art and a roster of names from Edwin Austin Abbey to Rufus Zogbaum, original art is available by such greats as Howard Pyle, N.C. Wyeth, Charles Dana Gibson, James Montgomery Flagg, Dean Cornwell, J.C. Leyendecker, Norman Rockwell, John Held, Jr., F.R. Gruger, Henry Raleigh, Haddon Sundblom, Joseph Clement Coll and hundreds of others.

Our pricing is realistic. For consignors we charge only a 25% commission on the selling price. For buyers, prices reflect both a low commission and a low overhead. We are out in South Norwalk, Connecticut, but only an hour by train or car from mid-Manhattan. We also enjoy looking at art. Bring us your pieces for appraisal, consignment or sale, either individual pictures or entire estates. If you are building your own collection we'll help you find what you want, even if we don't have it ourselves. We also publish the ILLUSTRATION COLLECTORS NEWS-LETTER to which you can subscribe for $7.50 a year. A sample copy is available for $2.00. Write to:

Walt or Roger Reed
Illustration House, Inc.
53 Water Street
South Norwalk, Connecticut 06854
Telephone: (203) 838-0486

R. F. Zogbaum

ILLUSTRATION HOUSE, Inc.

RAPIDOGRAPH®

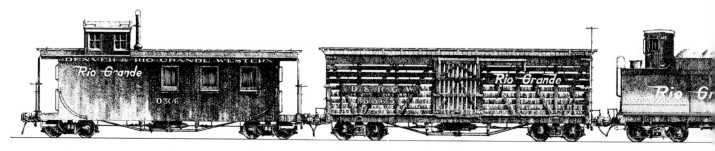

ART
... and the romance of the iron horse

"Thanks much," says James Young, "for giving me a way to express my interest in preserving some history in the steam locomotive." Artist Young is referring to the Rapidograph technical pen he used to create the strength and beauty in these drawings. The pen, he reports, is the one he purchased during his college days in 1965; The nib has been replaced from time to time "and the holder may look a little ragged, but the pen is still in everyday use."

Mr. Young has perfected the technique of "shaping" and "texturing" his subject matter with a highly developed, precision pointillism. His artistic recording of old steam locomotives includes commissions from historical groups and the private collections of railroad companys and individuals. So it is understandable that he says his art has been good to him, "and it would not have been possible to achieve, either for style or volume, without the dependability of the Rapidograph technical pen."

Dependability and ease of performance are the reasons Rapidograph pens are the most widely used technical pens in the United States and Canada. The patented DRY DOUBLE-SEAL™ cap keeps ink throughout the balanced ink-flow system fluid and clog-free for instant startup and optimum drawing time. No maintenance-plagued gimmicks for sealing or humidifying.

For the satisfaction of time well spent with any pen-and-ink drawing technique, be sure you see *Koh-I-Noor Rapidograph* on the pen. Accept no substitutes. "Get-acquainted" packaging (product No. 3165-BX) offers a special saving with pen/ink combination. Ask your dealer or send the coupon for details to Koh-I-Noor Rapidograph, Inc., Bloomsbury, NJ 08804 (201) 479-4124. In Canada: 1815 Meyerside Dr., Mississauga, Ont. L5T 1B4 (416) 671-0696.

These drawings by James Young are copyrighted by the artist and may not be reproduced for any reason without written permission from the artist.

KOH-I-NOOR
RAPIDOGRAPH®

Koh-I-Noor Rapidograph, Inc., 100 North St.,
Bloomsbury, NJ 08804 (201) 479-4124

In Canada: 1815 Meyerside Dr.,
Mississauga. Ont. L5T 1B4 (416) 671-0696

Please send complimentary Catalog "E" describing Rapidograph technical pens, Koh-I-Noor and Pelikan inks and other artist materials.
☐ Please send me the names of Koh-I-Noor dealers in my area.

_____
Name (Please print or type)

_____
Company Name if the following is a business address

_____
Number and Street, RD and Box, etc.

_____
City   State   Zip

©1982 by Koh-I-Noor Rapidograph, Inc.
® RAPIDOGRAPH is a Registered Trademark of Koh-I-Noor Rapidograph, Inc

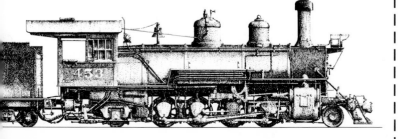

Illustrations by the
Artist: Raymond Kursar

To view Portfolio or to arrange for a Slide Presentation
Call or write to Raymond Kursar—One Lincoln Plaza
New York, N.Y. 10023 (212) 873-5605
See former ads in Illustrators Annuals 18, 19, 20, 21, 22, 23.

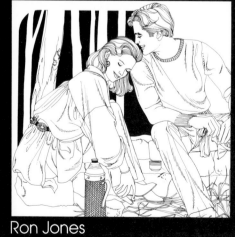

"BIG BEN, THE DRILLER"
EXHIBITED AT THE STAATLICHE KUNSTHALLE BERLIN
"ART AND CULTURE OF THE AMERICAN LABOR MOVEMENT"
MARCH 13th–APRIL 24th, 1983

BARNETT PLOTKIN 230 E. 44 ST., N.Y., N.Y. 10017 (212) 661-7149

KIRCHOFF/WOHLBERG
Artists Representative

433 E. 51 St., New York, NY 10022   212•644•2020

897 Boston Post Rd., Madison, CT 06443   203•245•7308

THE RODEO PAINTED

AN EXHIBITION

OUR TEN COMMANDMENTS of ARTIST REPRESENTATION

1. We represent only artists we believe in and are totally committed to them.

2. We believe in being more than agents and become involved in the *total career* of the artists we represent.

3. We appreciate the problems of the artist and try, whenever possible, to alleviate these problems.

4. We also appreciate the problems of the art director: his client-agency relationship, tight deadlines and budget limitations and try to help him solve these problems whenever we can.

5. We believe in *full representation.* That means taking on only that number of artists that we can fully represent as well as insuring that each artist is non-competitive in style with other artists we represent.

6. We believe in giving *full service* to our artists and to the art director, promptly and professionally. Every client, no matter what the job price, deserves the very best we can offer.

7. We believe in being *flexible.* Business conditions change. The economy rises and falls. Accounts switch. We and our artists must adjust to all changes in order to successfully survive.

8. We believe in always meeting deadlines and always keeping a bargain. We and our artists are only as good as our word and our last job.

9. We believe in *BEING HONEST* at all times. With our artists. With the art director. With ourselves.

10. And finally, we believe in our *profession...* the profession of representing artists. We firmly believe that it is the most exciting and challenging profession anywhere and we are proud to be a part of it.

Barbara Gordon
Associates Ltd.
165 East 32 Street
New York, N.Y. 10016
212-686-3514

Whistle In the Graveyard cover illustration by Nancy Munger © 1982 Viking Penguin, Inc.

Arts for the reproduction media
Representing Mark English, Bar
Jo Sickbert, George Carlson, Steve
Doug Pierson, and other leading

Since 1945, The **Joint Ethics Committee** has served the Graphics Industry by providing an alternative to litigation in the settlement of ethic disputes through peer review, mediation and arbitration.

Our five sponsors are the most respected professional organizations in the field: Society of Illustrators, Inc.; The Art Directors Club, Inc.; American Society of Magazine Photographers, Inc.; Society of Photographer and Artist Representatives, Inc.; The Graphic Artists Guild, Inc.

Selected representatives from these organizations serve as volunteers on the Committee. The services of the **JEC** are offered free of charge.

The **Joint Ethics Committee** has formulated a Code of Fair Practice which outlines the accepted ethical standards for the Graphics Industry.

To purchase the Code booklet for $2.50 or for further information please write to:

JOINT ETHICS COMMITTEE
P.O. Box 179, Grand Central Station
New York, NY 10163.